Ezekiel's Vision

The Living Creatures Revealed

by

Ingrid Bergner

The McDougal Publishing Company

All Scripture references are from the Authorized King James Version of the Bible, unless otherwise noted.

PUBLISHED BY:

The McDougal Publishing Co.
P.O Box 3595
Hagerstown, MD 21742-3595

ISBN 1-884369-06-5

Printed in Canada
For Worldwide Distribution

Table of Contents

Now it came to pass in the thirtieth year, in the fourth month, in the fifth day of the month, as I was among the captives by the river of Chebar, that the heavens were opened, and I saw visions of God.

In the fifth day of the month, which was the fifth year of king Jehoiachin's captivity, The word of the Lord came expressly unto Ezekiel the priest, the son of Buzi, in the land of the Chaldeans by the river Chebar; and the hand of the Lord was there upon him.

And I looked, and, behold, a whirlwind came out of the north, a great cloud, and a fire infolding itself, and a brightness was about it, and out of the midst thereof as the colour of amber, out of the midst of the fire. Also out of the midst thereof came the likeness of four living creatures. And this was their appearance; they had the likeness of a man. And every one had four faces, and every one had four wings. And their feet were straight feet; and the sole of their feet was like the sole of a calf's foot: and they sparkled like the colour of burnished brass. And they had the hands of a man under their wings on their four sides; and they four had their faces and their wings. Their wings were joined one to another; they turned not when they went; they went every one straight forward.

As for the likeness of their faces, they four had the face of a man, and the face of a lion, on the right side: and they four had the face of an ox on the left side; they four also had the face of an eagle. Thus were their faces: and their wings were stretched upward; two wings of every one were joined one to another, and two covered their bodies. And they went every one straight forward: whither the spirit was to go, they went; and they turned not when they went. As for the likeness of the living creatures, their appearance was like burning coals of fire, and like the appearance of lamps: it went up and down among the living creatures; and the fire was bright, and out of the fire went forth lightning. And the living creatures ran and returned as the appearance of a flash of lightning.

Now as I beheld the living creatures, behold one wheel upon the earth by the living creatures, with his four faces. The appearance of the wheels and their work was like unto the colour of a beryl: and they four had one likeness: and their appearance and their work was as it were a wheel in the middle of a wheel. When they went, they went upon their four sides: and they turned not when they went. As for their rings, they were so high that they were dreadful; and their rings were full of eyes round about them four.

And when the living creatures went, the wheels went by them: and when the living creatures were lifted up from the earth, the wheels were lifted up. Whithersoever the spirit was to go, they went, thither was their spirit to go; and the wheels were lifted up over against them: for the spirit of the living creature was in the wheels. When those went, these went; and when those stood, these stood; and when those were lifted up from the earth, the wheels were lifted up over against them: for the spirit of the living creature was in the wheels.

And the likeness of the firmament upon the heads of the living creature was as the colour of the terrible crystal, stretched forth over their heads above. And under the firmament were their wings straight, the one toward the other: every one had two, which covered on this side, and every one had two, which covered on that side, their bodies. And when they went, I heard the noise of their wings, like the noise of great waters, as the voice of the almighty, the voice of speech, as the noise of an host: when they stood, they let down their wings.

And there was a voice from the firmament that was over their heads, when they stood, and had let down their wings. And above the firmament that was over their heads was the likeness of a throne, as the appearance of a sapphire stone: and upon the likeness of the throne was the likeness as the appearance of a man above upon it. And I saw as the colour of amber, as the appearance of fire round about within it, from the appearance of his loins even upward, and from the appearance of his loins even downward, I saw as it were the appearance of fire, and it had brightness round about. As the appearance of the bow that is in the cloud in the day of rain, so was the appearance of the brightness round about.

This was the appearance of the likeness of the glory of the Lord. And when I saw it, I fell upon my face, and I heard a voice of one that spake.

— Ezekiel 1

Acknowledgements

First and foremost, a special acknowledgement and thanksgiving to the Lord Jesus Christ, Who laid His hand upon me and revealed to me His Word concerning Ezekiel's vision as recorded in this book. Without the revealing power of the Holy Ghost, I would never have known the divine truths that are recorded here. All glory to Jesus!

Allow me to thank Alice Schultz who, willing to invest many hours, asked me if she could type the messages that had been recorded on tape, as I had ministered on the first chapter of Ezekiel. God bless her for her foresight and willingness to bring forth God's will in my life and yours, as you read this book.

Then, there was Lynn McPhee (not her name now) who was willing to bring forth from those type-written pages a manuscript; but was unable to fulfil her vision.

But then I give special thanks to Gaylene Derkach who laboured long hours to bring forth the first manuscript.

I must mention Rev. Wallace Heflin who carried the manuscript to Virginia that it might be put into book form.

I cannot forget Gina Ordonez who has gone through the second manuscript, spending many hours and also Rose Romaniuk, our secretary at Faith Temple, who has typed that which I have corrected, as I have tried to bring forth that portion of the revelation which God would want recorded.

Last but not least, a most heartfelt thank-you to all the saints of Faith Temple, Winnipeg, Canada, for their prayers for their pastor, and for their help financially in order that God might have His revelation of the first of Ezekiel's visions in this book.

To God be all the glory! Amen.

Introduction

When most people speak about the Prophecy of Ezekiel, they usually make reference to the valley of dry bones (Ezekiel 37:1-14), or the waters running out from under the door of the sanctuary (Ezekiel 47:1-5). However, the first vision Ezekiel received from God was a description of the likeness of the Four Living Creatures. He relates this vision in explicit detail: telling when and how it happened, where he was when it happened, as well as what he actually saw. It is absolutely impossible to clearly understand this vision without divine revelation. If you try to understand the vision of the Four Living Creatures with the natural mind, it could become obscured by human conjecture and speculation. Ezekiel understood what God showed him; only to the extent of that which God wanted to do in him through that vision.

God will always bring His Word to you, if you are willing to receive it, but only to the extent that He will use it in your life. Therefore, it is not our purpose in life to attain to knowledge for knowledge's sake. It is, however, our purpose in life to attain unto the knowledge of God so that God might work through you and me. Thus, when God shares His knowledge with you, it is simply so that the knowledge shall become He, Himself, in you. Praise the Lord!

In the beginning was the Word, and the Word was God. John 1:1

He is still that Living Word. When He shares that Living Word, which is written in Scripture, with us, then that which is written becomes a part of us, and becomes the Living Word within us.

Over thirty years ago, God prophesied over me concerning the revelation of the Book of Ezekiel while I was attending a camp meeting near Vancouver, B.C., in July, 1959. Dr. Poole had taught two hours on the Book of Ezekiel, beginning with the Living Creatures and concluding with the Vision of the Temple. I had written down a few notes and was inspired, with a real hunger to hear more about Ezekiel. I was disappointed, therefore, when, on the third night, he began speaking about David and never returned to the Book of Ezekiel.

Before I left the camp meeting, God used the prophetic ministry of three men of God — Pastor Reg Layzel from British Columbia, Dr. David Schock from California, and Dr. Fred Poole from Pennsylvania — to prophesy over me. Along with other promises, God said that if I would meditate on the Word that I had learned while at camp, He would increase the Word within me and make it a "mighty river of revelation" flowing through me.

When I arrived in Winnipeg, I sat down at Eaton's Carpark, where I worked, took out my Bible and my scribbled notes, and said, "Well, Lord, here it is. I don't know what I can study from this, but at least I'll begin to read it and begin to really meditate upon what I learned at camp. And as I began, God's Spirit came upon me, and His Presence came and stood beside me. THIS WAS THE BEGINNING OF THE REVELATION OF THE LIVING CREATURES!

I first spoke on the Book of Ezekiel in February of the following year. I began to teach by faith that God would confirm His promise to me. He did. One night a week I taught on Ezekiel for a whole year, and I never got past the first chapter. (In every Bible I have used since then, the most worn pages are those which contain the first chapter of the Book of Ezekiel.)

During the next year God gave me more and more revelation into the Book of Ezekiel. The first eleven chapters came to me in great detail.

My own life was thus enriched by the knowledge I was receiving. Every time I stood to minister a new anointing came upon me; and I knew that Jesus was there to further reveal His Word to and through me. Because of the Living Word the message is always new. May all the glory be unto Jesus!

As you read the words of this book, given to me by the Spirit of God, I trust that the God of Ezekiel will make Himself more real in your life. May the visions of Ezekiel become your own. If that is to happen, you must open your Bible and look at the Word of God. There is a depth of the Scriptures that can be received only through Seeing the Word. Try it, and you'll see what I mean.

Rev. Ingrid Bergner, D.D.
Winnipeg, Manitoba

Chapter I

The Circumstances of the Vision

Now it came to pass in the thirtieth year, in the fourth month, in the fifth day of the month, as I was among the captives by the river of Chebar, that the heavens were opened, and I saw visions of God.

Ezekiel 1:1

God is a good God, and He desires the very best for His people. Historically, however, when God's people have begun to stray from Him, He has always been forced to allow hardship to come to their lives, to remind them that they needed the Creator and were nothing without Him. Often this hardship took the form of oppression from an enemy.

Before any enemy was allowed to oppress God's people, He warned them many times. When they refused to listen and went on in their idolatrous ways, they forced His hand. During one such period in Old Testament times, both Israel and Judah were conquered and their people taken as prisoners of war.

In B.C. 722, Shalmaneser, King of Assyria, took Samaria and carried away the ten tribes of Israel captive into Assyria.

In the ninth year of Hoshea the king of Assyria took Samaria, and carried Israel away into Assyria, and placed them in Halah and in Habor by the river of Gozan, and in the cities of the Medes. For so it was, that the children of Israel had sinned against the Lord their God, which had brought them up out of the land of Egypt, from under the hand of Pharaoh king of Egypt, and had feared other gods, And walked in the statutes of the heathen, whom the Lord cast out from before the children of Israel, and of the kings of Israel, which they had made.   II Kings 17:6-8

God, in His faithfulness, kept sending prophets to warn Judah to repent, lest she face the same fate — but to no avail. During the reign of King Jehoiachin, the Lord sent Nebuchadnezzar, King of Babylon, and bands of Chaldeans, Syrians, and Moabites against Judah to remove this rebellious people out of His sight. This was the first mass deportation from Judah. It began in B.C. 605. Eight years later, in B.C. 597, King Nebuchadnezzar with his armies came up against Jerusalem.

And Nebuchadnezzar king of Babylon came against the city, and his servants did besiege it. And Jehoiachin the king of Judah went out to the king of Babylon, he, and his mother, and his servants, and his princes, and his officers: and the king of Babylon took him in the eighth year of his reign. And he carried out thence all the treasures of the house of the Lord, and the treasures of the king's house, and cut in pieces all the vessels of gold which Solomon king of Israel had made in the temple of the Lord, as the Lord had said. And he carried away all Jerusalem, and all the princes, and all the mighty men of valour, even ten thousand captives, and all the craftsmen and smiths: none remained, save the poorest sort of the people of the land. And he carried away Jehoiachin to Babylon, and the king's mother, and the king's wives, and his officers, and the mighty of the land, those carried he into captivity from Jerusalem to Babylon. And all the men of might, even seven thousand, and craftsmen and smiths a thousand, all that were strong and apt for war, even them the king of Babylon brought captive to Babylon.   II Kings 24:11-16

Ezekiel was among these prisoners taken captive to Babylon. He was only twenty-five years old. This young priest who served in the Temple in Jerusalem was taken from his home and from his ministry and was exiled to a strange land, hundreds of miles away, never to see again that treasured temple and that treasured city. For the next five years, until he was thirty years old, Ezekiel was simply another of *the captives by the River of Chebar*. Then suddenly, something happened that forever changed his life. *The heavens were opened* to him, and he *saw visions of God.*

Five years can seem like a very long time. During those five long years, we have no record of anything supernatural or spectacular happening to Ezekiel. No doubt he had begun to think, *I'll never minister again. Never!* But God always hears the prayers of His people. He had heard the prayers offered up by this young priest. He had heard the cries of all the captives. God always hears, but He answers in His time.

We often try to do things on our own, in our own time; and we never get the desired results. God's time is perfect. He is eternal. He knows all the past, the present and the future. He knows the perfect moment in which to act. Unless we can get into God's time, we may do a lot of unnecessary begging and pleading when we pray. When we ask Him to do that which is untimely, He graciously denies our request. His love demands that He deny us in such moments. He knows best. When God's time comes for His purposes to be fulfilled in you or in me, and we are ready for God to meet us, He is never late.

God's time came in Ezekiel's life. After five years of living among the captives, something happened on a certain day that changed his life forever. *The heavens opened,* and he *saw visions of God.* This is Ezekiel's introduction to the revelations he received from God. The revelations that follow, which span twenty-one years of Ezekiel's life, are the result of an open heaven and *visions of God.*

Ezekiel's heart was prepared to meet God. His mind was open to God; and, therefore, the heavens opened to him. He was a man of spiritual perception and he was destined to become a man of great power. But how did he become a man of great power? By seeing God:

"The heavens were opened, and I saw God." In what manner did Ezekiel see God? The Word of the Lord came to him. The Word of the Lord came as a "picture lesson", as a vision but it was the Word of the Lord. The portrayal of the vision that Ezekiel saw was the Word of God to Ezekiel — God's message to His priest in order to impart God's ability to Ezekiel that he become God's prophet.

I relate with the Prophet Ezekiel in the excitement of that day, for there is no greater thrill in my life than having Jesus come and reveal His Word to me by the Holy Ghost. May you also experience this thrill.

Ezekiel would never forget that moment. It was, he said:

> *In the fifth day of the month, which was the fifth year of king Jehoiachin's captivity,*   Ezekiel 1:2

That particular moment in time was unforgettable to Ezekiel because it was in that moment that the Word of the Lord came EXPRESSLY to him.

> *The word of the Lord came expressly unto Ezekiel the priest, the son of Buzi, in the land of the Chaldeans by the river Chebar; and the hand of the Lord was there upon him.*   Ezekiel 1:3

Expressly means *individually or personally.* When you get a package by express, it has your name on it, and it is for you alone. When *the Word of the Lord came expressly unto Ezekiel,* it had his name on it. It was a personal message from God to him. I believe this is the way God wants to give His Word to us: expressly, individually, and personally.

This doesn't mean that God favours one person above another. He is no respecter of persons. He is willing to speak to one and all. But He needs a willing ear. Two people can sit together in church. One of them may receive all that God is saying, while the other goes away empty. Since the Word of God is personal, each individual must open his or her heart to it, receive it, and obediently act upon it. Otherwise, it has no impact in their lives.

Ezekiel had a willing heart, and God sent His Word expressly to Ezekiel to prepare him for a great work He had for him to do. In the first chapter, he receives the vision; in the second chapter, God calls him; and, in the third chapter, God sends him to minister to his own people. The next thirty-three chapters of Ezekiel recount this ministry.

Chapter thirty-seven of Ezekiel contains the famous vision of the valley of dry bones. Israel had lost her liberty, her anointing, and her song. Her inhabitants were captive in a strange land. The *children of Israel* lived as slaves, without any rights or privileges of their own. They had nothing of that which they were accustomed to having at home. They were the dry bones in that valley.

When Ezekiel heard the voice of the Lord, asking: *"Do you think these bones can live?"* he could not venture a guess. *"Thou knowest!"* was all that he could manage to reply (Ezekiel 37:3).

God said to Ezekiel, *"Prophesy upon these bones, and say unto them, O ye dry bones, hear the Word of the Lord."* Ezekiel prophesied every word as God commanded, and those dry bones did live — when God breathed on them. They stood upright and formed a great army!

God said to Ezekiel, *"Son of man, these bones are the whole house of Israel"*. We are witnessing *the whole house of Israel* being brought back to their land today. God's Word, prophesied by Ezekiel, is coming to pass in our time. Hallelujah!

Because of Ezekiel's experience, we now know that dry bones *can* live. Today, God is sending this Word to the dry bones of the Church of Jesus Christ. He is challenging us, as He did Ezekiel, and asking: *Can these bones live?* We now know the answer. Of course they can live! God is life! Anything that He breathes upon can live. There is hope for the church, as well as Israel, in the closing days of the twentieth century.

And the hand of the Lord was there upon him.   Ezekiel 1:3

This is the first of many times Ezekiel declares that the hand of the Lord was upon him. It is the hand of the Lord upon us which turns around the difficult situations. It is the hand of the Lord upon us that brings to us His express Word for our lives at that particular moment. Because the hand of the Lord was upon him and because the Word of the Lord had come expressly to him, he began to realize that God was there to show Himself alive to this captive priest who had sought to faithfully serve Him.

And I looked. Ezekiel 1:4

You must *look* to see; you must *look* if you want to see something or someone. This is just as true in the natural sense as it is in the spiritual sense. If we are not aware of the fact that there is something to be learned, we never learn. When you keep your spiritual eyes open, you can expect to receive God's revealed Word. When you go to church expecting to learn something, or when you read the Bible expecting to receive something from God, you are not disappointed. If you keep your eyes open, expecting to see, you will see as Ezekiel saw.

Ezekiel became a man of unusual spiritual perception because of these simple facts: He recognized the hand of the Lord upon his life and kept his eyes open, expecting to receive revelations from God, expecting to see God. The Book of Ezekiel has forty-eight chapters. The other forty-seven would not exist if it were not for the realities experienced by Ezekiel in this first chapter. Ezekiel saw because he determined to look. Together, let us open our eyes now, as never before, to see the things which Ezekiel was privileged to see so long ago.   ✸

Chapter II

Pentecost Revealed

And I looked, and, behold, a whirlwind came out of the north, a great cloud, and a fire infolding itself, and a brightness was about it, and out of the midst thereof as the colour of amber, out of the midst of the fire.   Ezekiel 1:4

Because he was a priest, Ezekiel knew the Scriptures. When he saw *a whirlwind out of the north, a great cloud, and a fire infolding itself,* he immediately recognized the presence of the Holy One of Israel, He Who dwells *on the sides of the north* (see Psalms 48:2). This was the One Who led Israel in the wilderness, the One Who covered them with a cloud by day, so they did not need umbrellas or parasols, or even big hats, to keep out the heat of the sun. The presence of the cloud kept their clothes from wearing out for forty years. It protected them from the destructive infrared rays of the sun. This was the One Who was their fire by night so that they had no need of electric light, or fire to keep the wild animals away from the camp (Exodus 13:21-22; Nehemiah 9:12 and 21).

He had appeared to Moses in the burning bush, commissioned Moses to bring forth the children of Israel out of Egyptian bondage, introducing Himself as *"I AM that I AM"*. The same Jehovah, the Great I AM, appears to His priest, Ezekiel, in bondage in Babylon, not in a burning bush, but in whirlwind, cloud and fire.

Picture Ezekiel sitting by the River Chebar. No doubt, if Ezekiel was like one of us, this revelation came at a time when he was least expecting it, perhaps even on a day when he was really wondering *when, if ever*, they would get back to Jerusalem, and *what* was God doing with them; and *what* was God doing with *him* sitting there among the captives? It was at this time that *"THE HEAVENS OPENED and he saw VISIONS OF GOD"*.

When the apostles said to Jesus, *"Lord, wilt thou restore again the kingdom to Israel?"* He replied to them:

> *It is not for you to know the times or the seasons, which the Father hath put in his own power. But ye shall receive power, after that the Holy Ghost is come upon you: and ye shall be witnesses unto me both in Jerusalem, and in all Judea, and in Samaria, and unto the uttermost part of the earth.*   Acts 1:7-8

Then Jesus told them to wait in the City of Jerusalem until they were *"endued with power from on high"* (Luke 24:49). Ezekiel, the priest whom God had ordained to become a prophet to his own people, needed the same power and anointing of God that the apostles needed many centuries later to fulfil the commission of Jesus Christ. Ezekiel tells us that he saw *"visions of God"*, and then he states:

> *... behold, a whirlwind came out of the north, a great cloud, and a fire infolding itself, and a brightness was about it, and out of the midst thereof as the colour of amber, out of the midst of the fire.*
>   Ezekiel 1:4

Ezekiel actually saw the God of Pentecost! Read about the One Who would baptize with the Holy Ghost and fire:

> *And when the day of Pentecost was fully come, they were all with one accord in one place. And suddenly there came a sound from heaven as of a rushing mighty wind, and it filled all the house where they were sitting. And there appeared unto them cloven tongues like as of fire, and it sat upon each of them. And they were all filled with the Holy Ghost, and began to speak with other tongues, as the Spirit gave them utterance.* Acts 2:1-4

The same phenomenon Ezekiel experienced in that whirlwind from *the north* was experienced by the apostles in that mighty rushing wind from *heaven*. The sound of the mighty rushing wind came from heaven, and from the north (the abode of God: Psalms 48:2), just as the whirlwind that Ezekiel saw. Ezekiel saw *a whirlwind* from *out of the north, a great cloud, and a fire infolding itself.* The *whirlwind* is parallel to the *mighty rushing wind* on the Day of Pentecost, *the great cloud* is parallel to *the Holy Ghost,* and *the fire infolding itself* is parallel to *the fire of the Holy Ghost.*

Prior to Pentecost, Jesus breathed on His disciples, saying, *"Receive ye the Holy Ghost"* (John 3:5). Then, *"when the day of Pentecost was **fully come"**,* the Holy Ghost came upon the disciples:

> *And there appeared unto them cloven tongues like as of fire, and it sat upon each of them. And they were all filled with the Holy Ghost.*

When the Holy Ghost came, He sat upon them, He covered them and filled them. Therefore, the Scriptures use the term, *"baptize with the Holy Ghost"* (John 1:33) because the Holy Ghost comes upon us, covers us, and fills us completely. Just as we are covered and immersed in the waters of baptism, so we are covered and immersed in the Holy Spirit when Jesus baptizes us with *"the Holy Ghost and fire"* (Luke 3:16).

Every person that is born again has received the Holy Spirit. When we are born of the Spirit (John 3:6), we receive the Holy Spirit inside of us; otherwise, we are none of His (Romans 8:9). Picture a glass of water which is almost filled but is not full to the brim. Many born again Christians only have this measure of the Holy Ghost inside of them, yet they are vibrant and radiant with the life of Christ. Sometimes they may show forth more of Jesus than some people who have been completely filled with the Holy Ghost, yet have neglected to continue being filled and transformed by the Spirit of Christ.

Other Christians have allowed the Holy Ghost to penetrate only a small part of their lives. Within their vessels, they only show water to the quarter or the half-way line. But they can be totally immersed in the Holy Ghost, in the same way that one can submerge a partially filled glass into a tank of water. Just as the water then covers the glass and rushes into it to fill it completely, so the Holy Ghost covers and fills us when we are submerged in Him. This is what Jesus does when He baptizes us with the Holy Ghost. He pours out upon us the Holy Ghost, who begins to cover us and come into us, so that we get so filled we can no longer contain Him.

When this happens, the Holy Ghost begins to pour out from us. We are covered outside and inside, and are so immersed in the Holy Ghost that He begins to pour out over the brim, and we begin to speak in other tongues as the Spirit gives the utterance! The last uncontrollable member, the tongue (see James 3:8), has been taken over by the Holy Ghost.

When you were born again, you received Jesus Christ into your being just as truly as Mary received the Word of God into her being. You also received the Spirit of God into your being. Everyone that is born again has the Spirit of God. If you don't have the Spirit of God in you, you are not born again.

Ezekiel saw *a fire infolding itself.* The fire of the Holy Ghost that appeared to the disciples as *tongues of fire* is the same fire of the Holy Ghost that appeared to Ezekiel as *a fire infolding itself.* When we receive Jesus Christ as our Saviour, we receive the fire of God; but when we are baptized with the Holy Ghost, the Holy Ghost immerses Himself within us and He enfolds Himself. Picture a handkerchief: in order to enfold the handkerchief, we wrap the handkerchief around itself, and then it automatically enfolds itself. When we are baptized with the Holy Ghost, He enfolds Himself in us as *a fire infolding itself.* He wraps Himself around Himself — because He is already in us; yet He now comes in greater measure. Each of us needs to be baptized with the Holy Ghost and with fire.

When I was baptized with the Holy Ghost, I began to shake. At first it frightened me. I didn't know what was happening. A dear saint who was present recognized what was happening to me and whispered in my ear, "It's just Jesus. You're not afraid of Him, are you?"

"No," I answered. Then I kept repeating her words of encouragement to myself. "It's just You, Jesus. I'm not afraid of You." And, although I kept shaking like a leaf, I was no longer afraid.

As my vessel got more and more submerged in the Holy Ghost, a wonderful thing began to happen. Something started flowing into me, just like water into a submerged vessel. I began to feel on the inside what I had been feeling on the outside. The Holy Ghost was flowing in. The water was rising. I was submerged in the glory of God. When the water rose to the top, the Holy Ghost overflowed, and I began to speak with other tongues — as He took control of my tongue, the most unruly member of the body.

The Spirit was already at work in my life; but through the baptism of the Holy Ghost, He covered Himself; He immersed Himself; He enfolded Himself. And from the midst of this fire of the Holy Ghost emerges the beauty of the Christ, the colour of amber.

Nobody has this experience and emerges bad tempered. It is impossible. When you are baptized with the Holy Ghost the beauty of amber comes forth from your life, the beauty of Jesus. When you are baptized with the Holy Ghost a sweet aroma comes forth from your life. You have a sweet taste in your mouth. You have been immersed in Jesus.

I personally knew only one of the people who were present when I was baptized with the Holy Ghost; but I loved them all. That is what the Holy Ghost does for you. He makes you love everybody. That is the beauty of the Christ, the beauty of amber.

When the Holy Ghost was outpoured on the Day of Pentecost, the apostles were empowered to do the works that Jesus had done. Because they believed Him, it happened to them exactly as He had said to them:

Verily, verily, I say unto you, He that believeth on me, the works that I do shall he do also; and greater works than these shall he do; because I go unto my Father. And whatsoever ye shall ask in my name, that will I do, that the Father may be glorified in the Son.

John 14:12-13

Ye shall receive power after that the Holy Ghost is come upon you: and ye shall be witnesses unto me.   Acts 1:8

Peter was a transformed man! And so were all the disciples of Jesus. They went out changed by the fire of God, filled with the power of God. They expected to do the same works that Jesus had done. And they did them!

Peter and John went up together to the Temple to pray. A certain man, lame from his mother's womb, was carried and laid daily at the Beautiful Gate. He had sat there all the time that Jesus passed by, but he had not been healed. But now he asked Peter and John for alms. They fastened their eyes on him and told him to look at them. As he did, he expected to receive something.

Then Peter said, Silver and gold have I none; but such as I have give I thee; In the name of Jesus Christ of Nazareth rise up and walk. And he took him by the right hand, and lifted him up; and immediately his feet and ancle bones received strength.   Acts 3:6-7

Peter and John had something to give. The power of God ministered life through them to the crippled man; and he went walking, and leaping and praising God (Acts 3:8). That's what faith and obedience to the Word of God will do for you.

When God first sent the Holy Spirit, those who were witness to what was happening could not understand and asked, *"What meaneth this?"* Peter, in answering them, quoted from the prophecy of Joel:

And they were all amazed, and were in doubt, saying one to another, What meaneth this? Others mocking said, These men are full of new wine. But Peter, standing up with the eleven, lifted up his voice, and said unto them, Ye men of Judaea, and all ye that dwell at Jerusalem, be this known unto you, and hearken to my words: For these are not drunken, as ye suppose, seeing it is but the third hour of the day. But this is that which was spoken by the prophet Joel; And it shall come to pass in the last days, saith God, I will pour out of my Spirit upon all flesh: and your sons and your daughters shall prophesy, and your young men shall see visions, and your old men shall dream dreams: And on my servants and on my handmaidens I will pour out in those days of my Spirit; and they shall prophesy: And I will shew wonders in heaven above, and signs in the earth beneath; blood, and fire, and vapour of smoke: The sun shall be turned into darkness, and the moon into blood, before that great and notable day of the Lord come: And it shall come to pass, that whosoever shall call on the name of the Lord shall be saved.   Acts 2:12-21

The prophecy of Joel was fulfilled on the Day of Pentecost in one sense. In another sense, it is still being fulfilled in all those who open their hearts to God to be filled with His Spirit. And it will yet be fulfilled completely in the last days. This is the day in which we must not be satisfied just to be baptized with the Holy Ghost. We must expect to see signs following our personal lives and our ministries. We must expect to be part of a great army which God is raising up.

Ezekiel not only saw Pentecost; he saw the results of Pentecost, the army of God that would go forth upon the earth. He saw activity, and he heard noise. I cannot imagine a quiet Pentecost. It's impossible. Activity creates noise. That bothers some people. They don't like noise; but I make no apologies. Power produces noise. Activity produces noise. That's just the way it is.

When people have a need, they don't mind the noise of our prayers for them. It is when people are self-satisfied that they complain about noise in the church. Even sinners don't mind the noise of Pentecost — if they want to find God. When God is working in your life, you don't care about what other people think or say. You're happy to be moving in God.

Many are offended when we speak with other tongues; but Peter was not offended. He said, *"This is that"*. If it is of God, why should we question? God can pour out His Spirit in the way He wants.

In the years 1946 to 1952, a restoration of spiritual gifts took place in the church. Many began to prophesy who had never even known what prophecy was before. This is a very real and supernatural experience.

Prophecy was never meant to replace or supersede the Word of God, but it does have an important place in the ministry. And God is not pleased when we ignore it or fail to give attention to what He is saying. Common courtesy demands that we listen carefully and politely to what He speaks to the Church.

Have you ever had the experience of talking to someone and knowing they were not listening to you? When that happens to me, I simply quit talking. I don't know what else to do. I believe that's also what the Lord does. He is not pleased with those who spurn His attempts to communicate.

There are many churches that actually forbid prophecy, tongues and interpretation of tongues. What a fearful thing to actually forbid God to speak in ways that He has chosen and placed within the Church for our edification! God has not changed His mind. He still wants a mighty army that will manifest His glory to the whole world. And the activity of that army will make noise.

Some people shout at their children when they expect to get action. Yet they resent it when the voice of authority is used in the church. God wants to give us a voice that both demons and people will obey, a voice of power and authority.

Many of those who have been baptized in the Holy Ghost treat Him only as a guest in the church. They put certain boundaries and limitations on what He can do. I once questioned why there was no opportunity given for an interpretation of a message in tongues in a conference of Pentecostal ministers. The answer was, "Because it was an evening meeting." Is God limited to morning meetings now?

Visitors do have limitations. They don't just barge into areas that have not been opened to them. A visitor in your home respects that home. If you are in your home, on the other hand, you feel free to do what you want. And that is the point. When God is moving in the church, He is in His own home. He should be free to do what He wants to do.

It is time for a new Pentecost. It is time for a new fire to burn within the Church. It is time for a new release of the power of the living God in our lives. Let the God of Ezekiel work in your life today.   ❀

Chapter III

Who Are the Living Creatures?

Howbeit when he, the Spirit of truth, is come, he will guide you into all truth: for he shall not speak of himself; but whatsoever he shall hear, that shall he speak: and he will shew you things to come. He shall glorify me: for he shall receive of mine, and shall shew it unto you. All things that the Father hath are mine: therefore said I, that he shall take of mine, and shall shew it unto you.   John 16:13-15

As a result of the baptism with the Holy Ghost, the Holy Spirit actually takes the things of Christ and shows them to us. We receive the things of the Lord because the Holy Ghost reveals the Christ to us. What did the Holy Ghost show to Ezekiel?

Ezekiel not only saw *a fire infolding itself,* but he also saw what came forth from the midst of the fire: *the colour of amber* and *the likeness of the four living creatures.*

> *... a fire infolding itself, and a brightness was about it, and out of the midst thereof was the colour of amber, out of the midst of the fire.*

Also out of the midst thereof came the likeness of four living creatures.   Ezekiel 1:4-5

Ezekiel saw, proceeding out of his visitation of God, *the colour of amber,* a reddish-yellow colour, similar to the light that proceeds out from fire. Jesus is *"the light of the world"* (John 9:5) and He, *"our God is a consuming fire"* (Hebrews 12:29). He is the One Who baptizes us *"with the Holy Ghost and with fire"* (Luke 3:16). *The colour of amber,* the mixture of the red fire and the yellow light, shows us the very beauty of Christ, the Baptizer. And out of our lives (as a direct result of the fire of God enfolding itself in us when we are baptized with the Holy Ghost), comes *the colour of amber,* the Christ nature, the Christ-likeness in our minds and emotions, in our bodies and in our spirits. The beauty of Christ will come forth.

"Also out of the midst of the fire came the likeness of four living creatures." Out of Pentecost came the Church of the Living God. The baptism with the Holy Ghost and fire not only reveals the Christ to us in the beauty of *the colour of amber;* but also causes the Christ to be revealed in and through us; therefore, in *the likeness of four living creatures* we see the ministry of the Christ in and through *the Body of Christ* and His Church.

Ezekiel does not say that he saw four living creatures; he says rather that he saw *the likeness of four living creatures.* In the living creatures we see the Christ; in *the likeness of the living creatures,* we see *the Body of Christ.* The Body of Jesus Christ is the likeness of Jesus Christ upon the earth. Ezekiel saw *the likeness of four living creatures,* and their appearance was as a man, not as an angel: *"And this was their appearance; they had the likeness of a man"* (Ezekiel 1:5). These living creatures should not be confused with the angelic beings called *seraphim* or *cherubim.* Although Ezekiel later calls these living creatures cherubim, he clearly identifies them as some particular and distinct creatures he saw by the River Chebar. God has created seraphim, cherubim, and angels in the heavens; but He also has His new creation on the earth, in *the likeness of a man,* and not an angel. Therefore, we are the likeness of the four living creatures, as the Body of Jesus Christ; made in His likeness.

For God, who hath commanded the light to shine out of darkness, hath shined on our hearts, to give the light of the knowledge of the glory of God in the face of Jesus Christ. But we have this treasure in earthen vessels, that the excellency of the power may be of God, and not of us. II Corinthians 4:6-7

We have the treasure of Christ in earthen vessels because God comes to live in us when we are born again. The beauty and the power of the Christ is to shine out from us. And therefore, the four living creatures, which represent Christ Jesus, have the likeness of a man. Through their faces, their wings, their feet, the hands of a man under their wings, and the four wheels that work with them, we will see the perfect creation of God that we are. The perfection of that new creation is what caused Jesus to say:

Verily, verily, I say unto you, He that believeth on me the works that I do shall he do also; and greater works than these shall he do; because I go unto my Father. And whatsoever ye shall ask in my name, that will I do, that the Father may be glorified in the Son. John 14:12-13

Paul states in Romans 8:28-29:

And we know that all things work together for good to them that love God, to them who are the called according to his purpose. For whom he did foreknow, he also did predestinate to be conformed to the image of his Son, that he might be the firstborn among many brethren.

You have become a child of God that you might be conformed to the image of Jesus Christ. It is for this purpose that *everything works together for good to them that love God.* To clearly understand Romans 8:28, we must realize that the ultimate purpose of God is for us to be made like Jesus. The Word of God states that *"tribulation worketh patience"* (Romans 5:3). How can tribulation work together for our good? By giving us patience. This is typical of the way God works things together in our lives for good, in order that we might become more like Jesus. When Ezekiel saw *the likeness of the four living creatures,* he actually saw us, as Spirit-filled Christians, come out of the phenomenon of Pentecost.

"The word of the Lord came expressly unto Ezekiel the priest." The vision that came to Ezekiel was the Word of the Lord, and it served God's purpose in preparing Ezekiel for his ministry to Israel. Another example of a vision used as the Word of the Lord is the Tabernacle shown to Moses on Mt. Sinai. When God decided He would have a tabernacle to dwell in, He made sure He gave a picture of that tabernacle to Moses. We would call it an architect's drawing, and that is exactly what God gave to Moses on the mountain. Once Moses saw the drawing of the Tabernacle, God said to him, *"Be sure you make it according to the drawing I showed you."*

> *Our fathers had the tabernacle of witness in the wilderness, as he had appointed, speaking unto Moses, that he should make it according to the fashion that he had seen.*   Acts 7:44

From the Tabernacle in heaven, which he saw in a vision, Moses drew up the plan for the Tabernacle on earth. God was the architect, and Moses was to follow the architect's plan carefully.

In Hebrews 12:22-24, we see the Living Original in heaven: Jesus, the High Priest of the New Covenant, the firstborn of many brethren.

> *But ye are come unto mount Sion, and unto the city of the living God, the heavenly Jerusalem, and to an innumerable company of angels, To the general assembly and church of the firstborn, which are written in heaven, and to God the Judge of all, and to the spirits of just men made perfect. And to Jesus the mediator of the new covenant, and to the blood of sprinkling, that speaketh better things than that of Abel.*

We must be made into the image of God's original in heaven, Jesus, the firstborn of many brethren. This transformation takes place as we become what we see in the Word of God, just as Ezekiel became what he saw. We become strong when we see strength in the Word of God; we become powerful when we see power in the Word of God; we become healthy when we see health and healing in the Word of God; we become loving when we see love in the Word of God. Just as Moses had to fashion the earthly Tabernacle according to the heavenly blueprint God showed him, God cautions us to be very sure we fashion ourselves like the pattern in the Living Word of God, which is Jesus Christ.

The Word of God is our pattern; it is the architect's blueprint, the drawing of the original in heaven, to ensure that our footprints are the same as His footprints. This is what Ezekiel is teaching us, for this is what Ezekiel was taught through his vision. He was taught the likeness of the Lord, and he actually became *the likeness of the living creatures.* He became like an eagle; he received the forehead of an ox; he became lion-like. He actually became these things, and more; he became the son of man to his generation, the man-face of the living creatures. God calls him *son of man* more times than Jesus Christ is called the Son of Man, so we know Ezekiel to be *the son of man.*

As we read this Word, we are going to become like this Word. As we see the Word of God, we are changed from glory to glory by the Spirit of the Lord:

> *Now the Lord is that Spirit: and where the Spirit of the Lord is, there is liberty. But we all, with open face beholding as in a glass the glory of the Lord, are changed into the same image from glory to glory, even as by the Spirit of the Lord.*   II Corinthians 3:17-18

This is the way we are changed; and this is why the Word of God came to Ezekiel, to change him. This is also why the Word of God comes to us, to change us. As we see the Word, we become the likeness of that Word. As we become the likeness of that Word, we are changed into His glory, *from glory to glory, even as by the Spirit of the Lord.* This is what the Word of God does for a person. As we see Jesus in His Word, the Word changes us so that we become in our earthly tabernacle like the Tabernacle in heaven. When we see the revelation of the four living creatures, we become more like JESUS CHRIST, because we see Him as He is.

In other words, we become *the likeness of the four living creatures.* We show forth what we already are in God. We are the Body of Jesus Christ, His likeness upon the earth.

Who are the living creatures? — the Body of Jesus Christ, which came into being through the glory of Pentecost.   ✸

Chapter IV

The Faces of the Living Creatures

The heavens were opened and I saw visions of God.

And I looked, and, behold a whirlwind came out of the north, a great cloud, and a fire infolding itself, and a brightness was about it, and out of the midst of it like the colour of amber, out of the midst of the fire.

Also out of the midst thereof came the likeness of four living creatures. And this was their appearance; they had the likeness of a man. And every one had four faces, and every one had four wings.

And their feet were straight feet;

And they had the hands of a man under their wings on their four sides; and they four had their faces and their wings.

As for the likeness of their faces, they four had the face of a man, and the face of a lion, on the right side: and they four had the face of an ox on the left side; they four also had the face of an eagle.

Ezekiel 1:1, 4-7, 10

We must always remember Ezekiel's statement in the very first verse of the book that records Ezekiel's vision of the Living Creatures: *"I saw visions of God."* In other words, let us see God, as we see the living creatures, and every part of this vision.

He saw the *"likeness of four living creatures"* — not six, not eight, but FOUR. Therefore, God used *the likeness of four living creatures* to portray Himself to Ezekiel, His priest, living among the Judean exiles by the River Chebar in Babylon.

God also used four men, anointed of the Holy Ghost, to portray His Son, Jesus Christ, to the world. Matthew shows the Messiah as the Lion, Mark as the Ox, Luke as the Son of Man, and John as the Son of God.

Always bear in mind that Ezekiel saw *the <u>likeness</u> of four living creatures.*

In the four living creatures we see Jesus Christ. In *the likeness of the four living creatures* we see the likeness of Jesus Christ, or the Christ-like ones, the Christians.

God also used four men, anointed of the Holy Ghost, to portray to the world the Christ-like ones. Paul springs forth into the Christian scene as the lion; Peter the submissive ox; James exhorts mankind to show forth Jesus Christ as a Man; and John highlights the Christians as sons of God.

There were *the likeness of four living creatures*, each living creature had four faces. Each living creature was identical.

> *And this was their appearance; they had the likeness of a man.*
> *And every one had four faces and every one had four wings;*
> *Their feet were straight feet;*
> *And they had the hands of a man under their wings on their four*
> *sides; and they four had their faces and their wings.*

"They had the likeness of a man," the Man, Christ Jesus, *"the Firstborn among many brethren;"* therefore, the likeness of the Body of Jesus Christ, the Church of the Living God.

> *But if our gospel be hid, it is hid to them that are lost: In whom the*
> *god of this world hath blinded the minds of them which believe not,*

lest the light of the glorious gospel of Christ, who is the image of God, should shine unto them. For we preach not ourselves, but Christ Jesus the Lord; and ourselves your servants for Jesus' sake. For God, who commanded the light to shine out of darkness, hath shined in our hearts, to give the light of the knowledge of the glory of God in the face of Jesus Christ. But we have this treasure in earthen vessels, that the excellency of the power may be of God, and not of us.
II Corinthians 4:3-7

In the faces of *the four living creatures,* we see Jesus Christ. Paul tells us, in II Corinthians 4, that we see the face of Jesus Christ in *"the glorious gospel of Christ"*. In fact, Paul says that *"God hath shined into our hearts to give the light of the knowledge of the glory of God in the face of Jesus Christ"*. In other words, we see the face of Jesus Christ in His Gospel, the Word of God.

Matthew shows the lion-face on the right side of the living creatures, the face of authority; at the same time, Mark shows the ox-face on the left side, the face of submission. On the front is the man-face, the face of humility; while on the back is the heavenly face, the eagle-face, or the face of majesty. Even as Luke shows Jesus as the Son of Man, John shows Him as the Son of God: front and back. It was *the likeness of four living creatures* that Ezekiel saw; and we must see that in His likeness, God was portraying the Christ-like ones. Just as it took four men, anointed by God, to portray Jesus Christ in the world, it took four men, anointed by God to portray the Christ in us. The gospels of Matthew, Mark, Luke and John declare to us the ministry of Jesus Christ as He walked and talked as a man upon this earth.

The epistles of Paul, Peter, James and John depict to us the ministry of the Christ-like ones, the Christians, as we live in this world. Just as Matthew portrays Christ as the King, the lion-face of authority, Paul shows the ministry of the Christian as the lion-face, our face of authority, victory, and kingliness. Predominantly, through Mark's gospel, we see the Christ as the Servant. Just as the ox is the beast of burden, serving men, so Jesus Christ is God's Servant, who has *"borne our griefs, and carried our sorrows"* (Isaiah 53:4). In his epistles, Peter exhorts us to "*submit ourselves*" to every ordinance of man for the Lord's sake: our ox-face. Just as Luke tells us the ministry of the Christ to His generation as the Son of Man, James also shows to us our ministry as the man-face in his epistle. The Gospel of John gives us the eagle-face of the Christ; the Son of God in the flesh, or the heavenly face. Listen to John as he begins his gospel: "*In the beginning was the Word and the Word was with God, and the Word was God.*" John mentions not a word about the lineage of Jesus. He simply shows that He was before all others. He is the Christ, the eagle-face, the heavenly face, the Son of God!

In John's epistles, the emphasis is on the eagle-face of the Christian.

The Book of Revelation portrays Christ and His Christ-like ones together forever in Heaven!

The Lion-Face

As we see the faces of *the four living creatures*, we must acknowledge that it took four men, anointed by the Holy Ghost, to bring the face of Jesus Christ to the world. Had Matthew not written his gospel, we would not see Jesus Christ as Matthew pictures Him: as the King. Matthew actually begins his gospel with the lineage of Jesus Christ, and continues with the Wise Men (Magi) questioning Herod, "*Where is He that is born King of the Jews?*" All through Matthew's gospel, we see one emphasis and one theme — that of the King. Just as the lion is the king of the animal kingdom, so the Lion of the Tribe of Judah, Jesus Christ, is the King of Kings. Even as Christ is King, we are kings. We have the face of a Lion. More people should show their right side, especially to the devil. There is none the devil fears more than the child of God who knows he has the face of the Lion of the Tribe of Judah. How frightened he is when you come toward him with that lion-face!

Paul knew this very well and emphasized it in all his epistles. He states in Romans 8:37:

> *Nay, in all these things we are more than conquerors through him that loved us.*

We are not intended to overcome in some things. We are intended to overcome in *all things* to be *more than conquerors*. We were victorious yesterday; we are victorious today; and we will be victorious tomorrow. We will be just as victorious two months from now as we were three weeks ago. We are victorious in all things through Christ. In Him, we are kings.

We all recognize that Christ is king, but few of us realize that we are also kings in Him:

> *And hath made us kings and priests unto God and his Father; to him be glory and dominion for ever and ever. Amen.*
>
> Revelation 1:6

I am a king. I have the face of a lion. I am determined to show that face to the devil. He fears the child of God who shows his face of authority. Satan flees when we approach him bearing the lion-face.

It is not enough to know that God portrays the Christ in the Scriptures, we must know that He portrays us, as well. The face of Jesus Christ is seen in the Scriptures, but our face is seen in the Scriptures too. We need to look in the looking glass of the Scriptures and see what we look like. Philippians 4:11-13 tells us:

> *Not that I speak in respect of want: for I have learned, in whatsoever state I am, therewith to be content. I know both how to be abased, and I know how to abound: every where and in all things I am instructed both to be full and to be hungry, both to abound and to suffer need. I can do all things through Christ which strengtheneth me.*

The Twentieth Century New Testament gives this rendering of the eleventh verse:

> *For I, however I am placed, have learnt to be independent of circumstances.*

The lion is not dependent upon circumstances. He is king, no matter what the circumstances. Nothing concerns him. Nothing makes him twitch an eyelid. He is king.

The Apostle Paul did not go around feeling sorry for himself when he didn't have enough to eat. Some might have said: "Lord, I must have been mistaken. If You had called me into the ministry, You would be supplying my needs." Paul was secure in the knowledge of Who God was and who he was in God. He knew what it was to be hungry; but he also knew that God never fails, and that if he remained strong in God, he would never fail either. He knew that he could *do all things through Christ.* ALL THINGS!

With confidence he continued his teaching to the Philippians.

> *But my God shall supply all your need according to his riches in glory by Christ Jesus.*   Philippians 4:19

God doesn't supply our need according to the status of our bank accounts. He is not limited by bank accounts. He has riches in glory. He never fails.

> *Now unto God and our Father be glory for ever and ever. Amen.*
> Philippians 4:20

The lion-face is steadfast. It expects to be the same forever.

Before Jacob died, he prophesied over his sons. To Judah he said, among other things, that he would be *as an old lion.* "*The sceptre shall not depart from Judah*" was God's promise to him (Genesis 49:9-10). That prophecy was, of course, fulfilled in Christ. The sceptre was an instrument of kingly authority.

The sceptre would not depart from Judah because he was *as an old lion.* You can't move an old lion. He has a mind of his own. He knows his importance. Nothing can intimidate him. God wants us to be like old lions. We are of the lineage of the Lion of the Tribe of Judah. We have those same kingly qualities in us. We must learn to be steadfast and unmovable.

> *Therefore, my beloved brethren, be ye stedfast, unmoveable, always abounding in the work of the Lord, forasmuch as ye know that your labour is not in vain in the Lord.*   I Corinthians 15:58

Judah was also said to be a young lion, *"a lion's whelp"* (Genesis 49:9). Young lions run around tearing everything up. They pounce on everything, and nothing escapes their attention. This is what we are to do to the works of Satan. We are destined to be a destructive influence toward the Enemy and his legions of demons. We must be both as the old lion, unmovable, and as the young lion, a potent force with which the world and Satan must reckon.

We must learn to be as steadfast, unmoveable and abounding in the work of the Lord as an old lion: and yet as busy as a lion's whelp tearing apart the works of the devil. This lion-face: the victorious, conquering, kingly face, should be the face that is always in us and shown through us.

The Ox-Face

To ensure that we have a good balance in this life, we have an ox-face: the face of a servant, the face of humility. Peter is the one God uses to show us the ministry of the Christian as the servant, as the ox-face. It is good and necessary to be balanced. Notice the living creatures. How very balanced they are: the face of authority on the right, the face of humility on the left; the face of man on the front, the face of the Son of God on the back. When you are balanced, you cannot easily be confused or deluded.

We need to have the ox-face, the servant face of humility, on the other side, balancing our lion-like natures.

Peter was used of the Lord to show us the ministry of the Christian as an ox-face, a humble face, a servant face.

> *Submit yourselves to every ordinance of man for the Lord's sake: whether it be to the king, as supreme; Or unto governors, as unto them that are sent by him for the punishment of evildoers, and for the praise of them that do well.*   I Peter 2:13-14

What we hear today among Christians is very different:

"I don't have to listen to him (or her)."
"God is my boss. I don't submit to anyone else."

We are called to submit to *every ordinance of man* and to do it *for the Lord's sake*. Peter went further:

Servants, be subject to your masters with all fear; not only to the good and gentle, but also to the froward. For this is thankworthy, if a man for conscience toward God endure grief, suffering wrongfully. For what glory is it, if, when ye be buffeted for your faults, ye shall take it patiently? but if, when ye do well, and suffer for it, ye take it patiently, this is acceptable with God. For even hereunto were ye called: because Christ also suffered for us, leaving us an example, that ye should follow his steps: I Peter 2:18-21

I am called of the Lord to *take it patiently* when I suffer for something good which I have done. We are so conscious these days of our individual "rights" that we sometimes get upset when someone gets after us — even when we have done something wrong. We are called not only to suffer when we are wrong. We are called to *take it patiently* when someone has corrected us when we haven't done anything wrong at all. That is the ox-face, the humble face. Jesus bore this face. He willingly suffered wrong for our sakes. We can do no less for Him.

Many Christians cannot get answers to their prayers and cannot be trusted with spiritual gifts because they don't have the ox-face. There is no telling what they would do with the knowledge of the word of knowledge and the wisdom of the word of wisdom. To operate the gifts of the Spirit effectively you must have the nature of Christ.

Jesus only did what the Father told Him to do. He only said what the Father told Him to say. He had no ulterior motive in anything that He did. His own will was laid aside, and He presented the ox-face. He lived a life of absolute submission. The lion-face is unbalanced without the ox-face.

What a miracle that Peter was used to teach about submission and humility! This is the man who cut off another man's ear just because he didn't do what Peter thought was right. He was a lion if there ever was one; but, thank God, he learned the balance of the lion and the ox.

The Man-Face

The living creatures had another face: *they four had the face of a man*. The lion-face was on the right. The ox-face was on the left. The eagle-face was on the back. And the man-face was on the front. This is the face that everybody sees, your neighbours and those with whom you work. James gave us good instruction:

> *Of his own will begat he us with the word of truth, that we should be a kind of firstfruits of his creatures. Wherefore, my beloved brethren, let every man be swift to hear, slow to speak, slow to wrath:*
> James 1:18-19

We are to be *swift to hear* and *slow to speak*. Most of us are just the opposite. We are poor listeners, and we answer quickly — without thinking much about what we are saying. In the Kingdom of God, however, there is no prize for a quick response, as there seems to be in the world today.

I was always slow to speak. My mother would get very exasperated with me. She was quick on the comeback. She would say to me (in Swedish), "By the time you think to say something, Ingrid, it's too late to say it." My slowness in answering was considered to be a hindrance. Even I considered it to be a hindrance. I would always think later, *I wish I had said this*; or *I wish I had said that*. Now I realize that a slow answer is a gift from God, and I thank Him for it.

The man-face of the Christian is *slow to wrath*. Don't imitate the quick-tempered ways of the world. Imitate Christ. He is *slow to wrath*.

> *For the wrath of man worketh not the righteousness of God.*
> James 1:20

When you get angry, you are not working the righteousness of God. You make hasty decisions and say things for which you are later sorry. If you want God's blessing to be on your life, get rid of that quick temper and be *slow to wrath*.

Wherefore lay apart all filthiness and superfluity of naughtiness, and receive with meekness the engrafted word, which is able to save your souls.   James 1:21

The greatest struggle in the Christian life is for control of the mind. If you are determined to follow the Lord, you must *lay apart* the filthy thoughts that keep your heart and soul in turmoil. You must lay aside your pride and receive God's meekness. Then you can begin to let His Word do its work in your life.

I once read a tract about meekness. It described it as being like plasticine. When a pebble is put into plasticine, it doesn't bounce back. It just stays there, losing its inertia. When you are meek, you don't react to outside influences in your life. Whatever happens, you keep praising God.

I love the book of James because it gives us such practical instructions about how to live the day-to-day life.

My brethren, have not the faith of our Lord Jesus Christ, the Lord of glory, with respect of persons. For if there come unto your assembly a man with a gold ring, in goodly apparel, and there come in also a poor man in vile raiment; And ye have respect to him that weareth the gay clothing, and say unto him, Sit thou here in a good place; and say to the poor, Stand thou there, or sit here under my footstool: Are ye not then partial in yourselves, and are become judges of evil thoughts?   James 2:1-4

If we act in response to whoever is around us, we will not get a heavenly reward. Some people do "extra things" when someone "special" is around. Otherwise they don't. True Christians are the same everyday, no matter who is nearby. They are not motivated by the clothing someone is wearing. They are motivated by the Spirit of God.

There are so many other practical teachings in James.

Ye adulterers and adulteresses, know ye not that the friendship of the world is enmity with God? whosoever therefore will be a friend of the world is the enemy of God. Do ye think that the scripture saith *in vain, The spirit that dwelleth in us lusteth to envy? But he giveth more grace. Wherefore he saith, God resisteth the proud, but giveth grace unto the humble. Submit yourselves therefore to God. Resist the devil, and he will flee from you. Draw nigh to God, and he will draw nigh to you. Cleanse your hands, ye sinners; and purify your hearts, ye double minded. Be afflicted, and mourn, and weep: let your laughter be turned to mourning, and your joy to heaviness. Humble yourselves in the sight of the Lord, and he shall lift you up. Speak not evil one of another, brethren. He that speaketh evil of his brother, and judgeth his brother, speaketh evil of the law, and judgeth the law: but if thou judge the law, thou art not a doer of the law, but a judge. There is one lawgiver, who is able to save and to destroy: who art thou that judgest another?*   James 4:4-12*

Be patient therefore, brethren, unto the coming of the Lord. Behold, the husbandman waiteth for the precious fruit of the earth, and hath long patience for it, until he receive the early and latter rain.
                                                              James 5:7

These are all demonstrations of our man-face as Christians. With God's help, this is the way we must learn to live.

The Eagle-Face

At the same time we bear the man-face, we also have an eagle-face. John, in his letters to the churches, shows us the eagle-face of the Christ and the eagle-face of the Christian.

Behold, what manner of love the Father hath bestowed upon us, that we should be called the sons of God: therefore the world knoweth us not, because it knew him not. Beloved, now are we the sons of God, and it doth not yet appear what we shall be: but we know that, when he shall appear, we shall be like him; for we shall see him as he is. And every man that hath this hope in him purifieth himself, even as he is pure.   I John 3:1-3

Can you see yourself as you read these words? You should be able to because you have a heavenly face, the eagle-face. God uses this side of your Christian life. You are from another kingdom. You are of royal parentage. Those who have this hope in them purify themselves by the Word of God. They work toward attaining the purity of Christ, so that they will be ready to meet Him.

If we did not know that these were different aspects of the same person, we would wonder if God was talking about someone else. These faces are so different. Yet they are all faces of the same person, Christ and Christ in us. This is a picture of you. Look at it carefully.

Beloved, believe not every spirit, but try the spirits whether they are of God: because many false prophets are gone out into the world. Hereby know ye the Spirit of God: Every spirit that confesseth that Jesus Christ is come in the flesh is of God: And every spirit that confesseth not that Jesus Christ is come in the flesh is not of God: and this is that spirit of antichrist, whereof ye have heard that it should come; and even now already is it in the world. Ye are of God, little children, and have overcome them: because greater is he that is in you, than he that is in the world.   I John 4:1-4*

The fourth face, the face on the back side of the living creatures is not a chicken face, nor an owl face. Chickens scratch up a lot of dust. Christians have no business doing that. Owls hoot and moan. The sounds they make are almost eerie. Some Christians have owl faces on the back side; but God wants us to have eagle faces.

Eagles fly very high. They soar in the heights. They love to go higher and higher. They make their nests in high places in the rock. They don't come down where they can be fenced in. If you are fenced in, God wants to set you free. He wants to give you the eagle-face. You were not designed for this world. You were designed for the high places. You were meant to stay up above all the concerns of life's daily circumstances.

Eagles are not bothered by storms. They simply fly higher — above the storms. Storms can be raging below them, and they are not even aware of it. God wants to lift us up above all principalities and powers.

God is not affected by the weather. He makes the weather. It cannot dictate to Him. It does His bidding. He is above the weather; and He wants us to live above the storms of life, as well.

When Jesus was asleep in the boat and the storm came up, the disciples were frightened. They wished He would wake up. Wasn't He concerned about them? But the storm could not disturb *His* rest. When the storm got worse and worse, until they finally thought for sure they would drown, in desperation they woke Him up. And when they did, He rebuked their lack of faith. Storms can't hurt the child of God. We live above the storms of life.

"Jesus," they called. "Wake up! We are about to perish. Don't You care?"

His serene answer was, *"Peace! Be still!"*

And that was it. All winds and contrary waves ceased. That is what you call an eagle-face.

Some Christians need a few more eagle feathers. They haven't learned to fly very high yet. They keep getting pulled down by the drafts of this world. They don't know yet what it is to soar free of every care.

We have an eagle-face! We are *of God* and have *overcome them.*

> *Herein is our love made perfect, that we may have boldness in the day of judgment: because as he is, so are we in this world.*
>
> I John 4:17

As He is, so are we. What a powerful fact! Can we grasp that truth? *As He is, so are we.* We have an eagle-face. Most Christians believe that we *will become* like Jesus Christ in Heaven, but the Bible says we are like Him *in this world.* We have an eagle face now, not just when we get to heaven. Don't wait for heaven to learn to fly. If you do, you may never get there. Learn to soar here and now.

> *There is no fear in love; but perfect love casteth out fear: because fear hath torment. He that feareth is not made perfect in love.*
>
> I John 4:18

I am an eagle. You are an eagle. You have an eagle-face *in this world.* Get up there in those higher currents. Don't be easily dragged down by the gravity of life. Let those higher currents lift you up so that you can soar free. As Paul wrote to the Corinthians:

> *Who also hath made us able ministers of the new testament; not of the letter, but of the spirit: for the letter killeth, but the spirit giveth life. But if the ministration of death, written and engraven in stones, was glorious, so that the children of Israel could not stedfastly behold the face of Moses for the glory of his countenance; which glory was to be done away: How shall not the ministration of the spirit be rather glorious?*   II Corinthians 3:6-8

Some people interpret this passage incorrectly. To them, it is the Word of God which is dead and which brings death to a service — as opposed to the Spirit, which brings life. That is a wrong interpretation. Paul was not talking about the Word of God, but about the Law. When God gave the Law to Moses, it spelled death to those who did not keep it. This is what he means by *"the letter killeth".*

However, there was something glorious about the Law. It was so glorious that when Moses came down from the mountain his face glowed so brightly that the people could not look directly at him.

> *And the children of Israel saw the face of Moses, that the skin of Moses' face shone: and Moses put the vail upon his face again, until he went in to speak with him.*   Exodus 34:35

Moses had been on the mountain in the presence of God for forty days and forty nights. During that time, God gave him a word that spelled death to those that did not keep it. But even that word, the Law, which God wrote with His own finger on tables of stone, was so glorious that the face of Moses shone, and He had to cover himself with a veil.

If that kind of word, which was written on tables of stone and which spelled death, could put such a shine on your face, how much more a word of grace and life, written in the fleshly tables of the heart! We have an eagle-face.

The Word of God is like a looking glass. When we look into it, we are changed. We do not have to bear the image of this earth. We can bear the image of the heavenly. We do not have to be confined to this world. We can soar with the eagles.

> *Grace and peace be multiplied unto you through the knowledge of God, and of Jesus our Lord, According as his divine power hath given unto us all things that pertain unto life and godliness, through the knowledge of him that hath called us to glory and virtue: Whereby are given unto us exceeding great and precious promises: that by these ye might be partakers of the divine nature, having escaped the corruption that is in the world through lust.*
>
> II Peter 1:2-4

Many people seem to believe that the message of today is for grace and peace to be subtracted from you. But that is not God's goal. He wants to add grace and peace to you. He wants to make you a partaker of the Divine nature. He can do that if you will feast on His Word.

Just as surely as God wrote the Law and Moses became a partaker of that Law — so much so that his flesh shone — we may become partakers of the Word, as we look into the glass. We may become partakers of the Divine nature.

This shows us that the faces of the Christian are not automatic. You have to put them on. If you read the epistles of Paul and do what they say, you will have a lion-face, and other people will see it. There will be a new authority in your life. If you read the letters of Peter and do what he teaches, you will have an ox-face. You will be submissive. If you read the letter of James and do what he says there, you will have a man-face to your generation, just as Jesus had to His. If you read the letters of John to the churches and do what he says, you will have an eagle-face. You'll learn to soar above the trials and tribulations of life.

During one of the greatest periods of heartbreak in my personal life, people would approach me and tell me that they enjoyed my company and looked forward to seeing my smiling face. They didn't see the heartbreak. They didn't see the trials and tribulations. I had learned to soar above the heartbreak. When they looked at me, they saw peace and joy. One wealthy woman told me that she would give anything to have what she saw on my face.

The secret to the eagle life is not that the eagle is so strong in himself. The secret is that the eagle knows how to get into those upward drafts. He knows how to let the winds of life be used to his advantage, to lift him up, rather than to destroy him.

If you look into the glass of God's Word long enough, that glory will be imparted to you. If you spend enough time in His Word, His nature will begin to form in you. Our problem is that we keep looking at ourselves as we are, rather than looking into God's Word, at what He intends to make us. We must believe God's image of us, not our own. We must stop arguing with God that we can never become what He has destined us to be. If we can just believe the Word, it has the creative power to make us what we are not — at present.

> *My son, attend to my words; incline thine ear unto my sayings. Let them not depart from thine eyes; keep them in the midst of thine heart. For they are life unto those that find them, and health to all their flesh.*   Proverbs 4:20-22

Let your *flesh* shine with the glory of God. Don't resist the Word. Receive it. Act upon it. It is then that the transforming power is unleashed. James said:

> *But be ye doers of the word, and not hearers only, deceiving your own selves. For if any be a hearer of the word, and not a doer, he is like unto a man beholding his natural face in a glass: For he beholdeth himself, and goeth his way, and straightway forgetteth what manner of man he was. But whoso looketh into the perfect law of liberty, and continueth therein, he being not a forgetful hearer, but a doer of the work, this man shall be blessed in his deed.*
> James 1:22-25

Once you catch a glimpse of what God intends for you, you cannot simply go away and forget the manner of person you should be. God is telling you that you have a face like Jesus on the right side; you have a face like Jesus on the left side; you have a face like Jesus on the front side; you have a face of Jesus on the back side. You are a lion; you are an ox; you are a man; you are an eagle. Don't ever forget it.

At the end of our journey through life, our perfected face will be revealed. The work of God's Spirit, writing His nature in our hearts will be manifest for all to see. At that time, He will write His name in our foreheads.

> *And there shall be no more curse: but the throne of God and of the Lamb shall be in it; and his servants shall serve him: And they shall see his face; and his name shall be in their foreheads. And there shall be no night there; and they need no candle, neither light of the sun; for the Lord God giveth them light: and they shall reign for ever and ever.*   Revelation 22:3-5

In that day, it will be known to all that we have the faces of Jesus. But we know it already.

Allow God to give you the face of Jesus — on every side.

Chapter V

The Wings of the Living Creatures

... and every one had four wings.
And they had the hands of a man under their wings on their four
sides; and they four had their faces and their wings. Their wings
were joined one to another; they turned not when they went; they
went every one straight forward.
... and their wings were stretched upward; two wings of every one
were joined one to another, and two covered their bodies. And they
went every one straight forward: whither the spirit was to go, they
went; and they turned not when they went.

Ezekiel 1:6, 8-9, and 11

Ezekiel was a very real person. He could write of such deep spiritual things because he put himself into a position to receive from God. A well is limited in the water it can hold by its depth. A vessel cannot hold more than its capacity. The more a vessel is developed, the more it can hold. The more you can expand your spirit, the more God can give you. Open yourself to the revelation of the wings of the living creatures.

The living creatures were spiritual beings. They needed wings to move about in the heavenlies. No earthly being can live in the heavenlies without first developing wings. When God portrays His Body, His people, He portrays them with wings because they are a heavenly, a spiritual creation. We are not creatures of the earth alone. We have a man in us that is from Heaven. In I Corinthians 15:44, we read about the spiritual man, as well as the earthly man:

> *It is sown a natural body; it is raised a spiritual body. There is a natural body, and there is a spiritual body. And so it is written, The first man Adam was made a living soul; the last Adam was made a quickening spirit. Howbeit that was not first which is spiritual, but that which is natural; and afterward that which is spiritual. The first man is of the earth, earthy: the second man is the Lord from heaven.*
> I Corinthians 15:44-47

Use the right terminology when you speak about the inner man. Remember, there was the first man, Adam; and Christ is the *last* Adam; not the second Adam, the last Adam. There is that first man, the earthy man that is created in your mother's womb. That man is *of the earth*. But when you are born again, you have a second man. This second man is heavenly. He is the Christ, come down to live in you. Just as surely as He came to live in Mary, He comes to live again in every born again person of God. This is the second man, and He is *the Lord from heaven*. He lives in you, and He is a spiritual man.

> *As we have born the image of the earthy, we shall also bear the image of the heavenly.*   I Corinthians 15:49

There is no father, that is a true father, that is not proud of the fact that his son looks just like him. Our Father, God, is certainly that kind of father. The more you look like His Son, Jesus Christ, the more proud He is of His creation.

We are predestined to bear the image of the heavenly, just as surely as we have borne the image of the earthly. This is God's will for our lives. Just as it is natural and expected for us to bear the image of our earthly parents, it is natural and expected that we should bear the image of our heavenly Father.

> *Now this I say, brethren, that flesh and blood cannot inherit the kingdom of God; neither doth corruption inherit incorruption. Behold, I shew you a mystery; We shall not all sleep, but we shall all be changed, In a moment, in the twinkling of an eye, at the last trump: for the trumpet shall sound, and the dead shall be raised incorruptible, and we shall be changed.*   I Corinthians 15:50-52

When this wonderful time comes, you will experience a profound change. But there is another change that must take place before this time. We need it now, not in the future. We need it now, not when we get to heaven. As we begin to see ourselves as heavenly beings (because Christ sees us as heavenly beings), we shall be changed into His image.

Be assured of the fact that God sees us as heavenly beings.

> *But God, who is rich in mercy, for his great love wherewith he loved us, Even when we were dead in sins, hath quickened us together with Christ, (by grace ye are saved;) And hath raised us up together, and made us sit together in heavenly places in Christ Jesus:*
> Ephesians 2:4-6

This passage is not in the future tense. This is a present reality. He *loved us.* He *quickened us together.* He *hath raised us up together.* He *made us sit together in heavenly places.* This is an accomplished fact. Let us begin to live in what God has already provided. The future in Christ will be wonderful, but we don't have to wait for the future. We can live heavenly lives *now.* We can sit in heavenly places *now.* We have wings. We can fly.

When God created the bumble bee, He gave it wings. According to all the laws of aerodynamics, the bumble bee should not be able to fly.

Its wing-span is not large enough in relation to its weight. But the bumble bee doesn't know that. All he knows is that God gave him wings, so he flies anyway — defying all the laws of nature and flying in the face of conventional wisdom.

Many people will say that you can't fly either:

How could you fly?
It is impossible.
You are human, after all.
You are a carnal creature.
Just accept your limitations.
You think you are sitting in heavenly places?

All of that may sound very reasonable. There may be one truth in the natural and a very different truth in the spiritual. What is important to us is the mind of Christ; and, in His mind, you can fly. Forget what people say and start flying. If God gave you wings, He knows that you can fly.

Your natural side may seem to weigh you down hopelessly. So does the body of the bumble bee. Your wings may seem to be much too small. So are those of the bumble bee. Yet it flies, and so can you. God gave you wings.

A chicken has a fairly broad wing-span and, theoretically, should be able to fly very well. But it can't. A bumble bee can out-fly a chicken any day. It is all in the desire, the determination, and the way you see yourself. Chickens fly only if they are forced to. They would rather scratch around on the ground. Bumble bees spend most of their time in flight. We rarely see them earthbound.

I believe God. He said that He has *raised us up together*. He said that He has *made us sit together in heavenly places*. I intend to take advantage of what He has provided for me. He gave me wings, so I am going to fly.

God has a purpose for each of our lives.

That in the ages to come he might shew the exceeding riches of his grace in his kindness toward us through Christ Jesus. For by grace are ye saved through faith; and that not of yourselves: it is the gift of God: Not of works, lest any man should boast. For we are his workmanship, created in Christ Jesus unto good works, which God hath before ordained that we should walk in them.

Ephesians 2:7-10

God has created us and made us a new and a spiritual creation, capable of sitting in heavenly places. He has given us the knowledge of His purpose and calling on our lives. Paul, conscious of God's design for the Ephesian people, prayed for them:

That the God of our Lord Jesus Christ, the Father of glory, may give unto you the spirit of wisdom and revelation in the knowledge of him: The eyes of your understanding being enlightened; that ye may know what is the hope of his calling, and what the riches of the glory of his inheritance in the saints, And what is the exceeding greatness of his power to us-ward who believe, according to the working of his mighty power, Which he wrought in Christ, when he raised him from the dead, and set him at his own right hand in the heavenly places, Far above all principality, and power, and might, and dominion, and every name that is named, not only in this world, but also in that which is to come: And hath put all things under his feet, and gave him to be the head over all things to the church, Which is his body, the fulness of him that filleth all in all. Ephesians 1:17-23

We were dead in sins, but He *quickened* us *together with Christ.* When Jesus rose from the dead, He had finished His work on the earth. Yet, before He ascended to the third Heaven to present the sacrifice of His blood on the Mercy Seat of Heaven, He stopped to let His disciples know that He was indeed alive. This was important because we are quickened together with Him. The same power that brought Him forth from the dead keeps us alive in Christ. This was the act that gave us wings.

Most of us would get very excited if someone told us there was a stick of dynamite under us set to go off. Yet the same power that raised Jesus from the dead is working in each of us, and we don't get very excited about that. This is more than a stick of dynamite. This is the limitless power of God. Get excited! Spread your wings!

Everyone gets excited about fast jets and faster spaceships, but the power of the fastest jets and spaceships cannot even be compared to the potential God has placed with us. We are heavenly creatures.

This is not just a religious theory. When we make God's truth our own, we begin to experience it. This is reality. Start flying. You have wings.

When the space technicians start to give the countdown at Cape Canaveral in Florida, everyone gets excited. Something is about to happen. An enormous, man-made rocket is about to ignite and thrust itself out of earth's orbit into space. That is exciting. But we have something much more exciting. We are not earth-bound either. We are heavenly. God began the countdown for us a long time ago. He is waiting for us to get excited and start expecting to take wing and lose our earthly limitations.

Giving thanks unto the Father, which hath made us meet to be partakers of the inheritance of the saints in light: Who hath delivered us from the power of darkness, and hath translated us into the kingdom of his dear Son: Colossians 1:12-13

And hath translated us ... : We are not only delivered from the power of darkness — all human inhibitions, all fear, all doubts, all the power of the devil — but we are also already translated into the kingdom of His dear Son.

Some of those lift-offs take a long time. A lift-off in the Spirit can take place in your life in moments. It doesn't take God long. He doesn't need the weeks and months of pre-flight preparation. He can lift you into the heavenlies just as fast as you can believe Him for it.

As the Scriptures aptly declare:

God is not a man, that he should lie; neither the son of man, that he should repent: hath he said, and shall he not do it? or hath he spoken, and shall he not make it good? Numbers 23:19

God is not a liar. Since He said that you are seated in heavenly places, you are. Since He saw you with wings, you have them. Believe Him. He wouldn't tell you to fly if you couldn't do it. He knows that you can do it through the power of the Holy Ghost given to you so that you can experience your potential in Jesus Christ. He said:

> But ye shall receive power, after that the Holy Ghost is come upon you ... .   Acts 1:8

Nobody goes to the airport and expects a plane to take off without power. The take-off demands the most power of all. Once you are in the air, it takes far less power to keep moving. That original thrust, needed to get the plane moving down the runway fast enough until the lift of the wings takes over, is immense. This is the most dangerous time of the flight. Oh, I wish every Christian had a more powerful take-off. We would have far fewer tragedies if there was more power for the launch.

I seldom tell all of my personal experience when I was baptized in the Holy Ghost for two reasons: (1) When we do tell our experiences, someone always gets the idea that they have to have the identical experience. And, since this is the baptism of the Holy Ghost, He does it as He wants to, not as we expect Him to. We cannot limit Him to one method. (2) Because my experience is not easily put into words. I had such a wonderful take-off in the Spirit. It was August 29, 1943.

That night, I was on my knees in the prayer room at Calvary Temple, Winnipeg, Manitoba, asking (beseeching) the Lord to fill me with the Holy Ghost. Such a hunger for more of God filled my soul. The same Holy Spirit that shook the house in which the believers were sitting on the Day of Pentecost came upon me, and I began to shake uncontrollably. As I reassured myself that this was Jesus, my fear left me, and God began to speak to me. His fist question was, "Will you take off your rouge and mascara for Me, Ingrid?" (God had been "working" on me along these lines for about seven months, with only partial success.) At that moment, with the power of God mightily upon me, what my face looked like didn't mean anything to me.

"Will you go home and tell your husband that you are saved?" I had never told my husband about my wonderful experience of salvation, when Jesus met me at our home, at a quarter to twelve midnight on Sunday, November 8th, 1942. My husband had declared that he would leave me if I ever let my attending church "get" me. At that moment, nothing and no one meant anything to me, except Jesus!

"Will you go out in My work for Me, Ingrid?" In the Pentecostal Church circles I was in, this was the usual terminology for going out in the ministry of the Lord. God knows how to make us understand what He is asking us to do.

To all these three requests of God, I answered, "Yes, I will." It was easiest to say "I will" to the last one of the three because I didn't know anything about the ministry that God had prepared for me. Oh! Hallelujah! I praise Jesus for every day I have been privileged to serve Him!

With my hands raised in surrender to the Lord, I fell backward, prostrate on the floor, unable to move except for moving my head sideways (I could not lift it up.), and my hands and arms lifted in praise to God.

Oh! What glory filled my soul! I began to speak with other tongues as the Spirit gave utterance. I had *joy unspeakable and full of glory* as I spoke in a language (languages that I did not understand and had learned). I laughed and laughed in the Spirit, so much so that my face was in a continual expression of laughter. For days afterward, my face felt strange if I brought it to its usual expression. I felt my stomach muscles for days because of laughing so long, lying flay on my back, unable to raise myself.

Then I was carried by the Spirit to a place far above the earth. I think of the Apostle Paul, when he said:

I knew a man in Christ above fourteen years ago, (whether in the body, I cannot tell; or whether out of the body, I cannot tell: God knoweth;) such an one caught up to the third heaven.

II Corinthians 12:2

Certainly my spirit was caught up out of the body to the second heaven.

I did not experience any *feeling* of being lifted up, or any *awareness* of being translated in my spirit. I simply found myself in the presence of Jesus in a *different* place. I had been taken up, above the ceiling of the prayer room (which was in the basement of the church), above the ceiling in the church, above the roof. Yet I could see through them all, through the walls, through the ceilings and through the roof. I had taken on one of those wonderful characteristics of Christ. Walls didn't stop Him, and doors didn't stop Him.

While my body was lying in the prayer room at Calvary Temple, my spirit was soaring in the heavenlies with Jesus. I don't know how high up I was. I can only say that the atmosphere was heavenly, one of iridescent glory. I was in the midst of fleecy, white clouds; and I seemed to be floating with them.

I remember looking down at my body on the floor and seeing those who were kneeling around me. I only knew one other person in the prayer room. It was only my second time to visit the room. I had fallen under the power and was flat on my back. But the thing that drew my attention was that my hat was tipped at a funny angle on my head. This struck me as being very funny. Like a woman, I was thinking: *Just look at that hat of mine.* The hat was blue and had a fuchsia-coloured ribbon around it. Perhaps a man would never have noticed his clothing; but, being a women, I still remember it vividly. The Lord didn't seem to mind my thoughts about myself on earth while I was experiencing such glory. Jesus is so very understanding. I love Him.

I didn't see Jesus; but I knew His presence was there with me. He made me to know that I could have anything I would ask Him for. There was nothing that He would deny me. I immediately said, "Lord, You will save Telly" (my husband); "and Jesus, You will save little Hughie" (my son was five years old at the time). "And, O Lord, for Papa ... Please save his soul." (My father was much opposed to the Gospel and had left home for a year and a half after my mother was baptized in water.) And then I said, "And, Jesus, You will look after Mama's eyes so that she doesn't go blind." (My mother had had poor eyesight ever since she was a child and had been told by an eye specialist some years before that there was nothing medical science could do for her vision; and it had increasingly deteriorated through the years, until now she faced complete blindness.)

My father gave his heart to Jesus on May 28th, 1944. My son prayed the sinner's prayer when he was twelve years old. My mother's eyes never dimmed any more from that time. She had the same amount of sight until she went home to be with Jesus in 1956. I had to wait until my husband passed away, in 1973, before I actually was assured by the Lord that He had answered my prayer for him.

At the exact time that my husband passed away in the hospital, God spoke to me at home. My husband had left home in 1953, ten years after my visitation with Jesus in the heavenlies; but my faith for his salvation had never wavered. Years had come and gone since that "glory night", August 29th, 1943; and now it was December 3rd, 1973. I had been visiting my husband in the hospital for about six weeks, since I learned of his illness on my return from my second overseas tour. My son had phoned and said, "Mom, Dad has only about two hours to live."

I was getting ready to drive to the hospital and praying at the same time, "You will heal Telly, Jesus; You will raise him up; You will save his soul."

Jesus answered me, "He is with Me."

I thought Jesus was *looking after* my husband, and he would be healed, for I knew God would save his soul. But, when I reached the hospital, I realized that God had already saved his soul, and my husband was indeed "with Jesus". Telly's salvation was confirmed by the Lord through two visions that God gave to two saints who did not even know him in this life. God is faithful!

I never thought to ask anything for myself, or anything material or financial, when Jesus transported my spirit into the heavenlies; but I did receive everything I asked Him for in the glory of His presence. His presence brings forth His will in our lives.

When we have such power at our disposal, we must get serious with God. He has entrusted this power to us. Let us use it wisely. Let us *redeem the time*. Let us operate with *understanding*. Let us be careful to know and do *the will of the Lord*.

And be not drunk with wine, wherein is excess; but be filled with
the Spirit;   Ephesians 5:18

Some Christians are saying that it is okay to drink wine — as long you don't drink too much. I think it is better to drink the wine of the Spirit. It can never harm us. The more you drink of it, the better. *Be filled with the Spirit.* Once you drink this wine, you won't want or need any other.

Our power needs to be regularly replenished. If those in charge of an aircraft did not give consideration to the need for refuelling the aircraft, we wouldn't have much confidence in them. The Bible commands us to *be filled with the Spirit.* After we are baptized in the Holy Ghost, we need to receive constant refillings. Those who do not take time for being refilled find themselves grounded. Since you are not running on your own power, you cannot run indefinitely without being refilled. Being filled with the Holy Ghost is just as necessary as refuelling an aircraft. And neglecting to be filled with the Holy Ghost has just as serious consequences. Make sure that you have enough for any given day before you take wing. You don't want to come crashing down suddenly.

Speaking to yourselves in psalms and hymns and spiritual songs,
singing and making melody in your heart to the Lord; Giving
thanks always for all things unto God and the Father in the name of
our Lord Jesus Christ;   Ephesians 5:19-20

We need to thank God for yesterday and all that happened to us; we need to thank God for today and all that happened to us; and we need to thank God for tomorrow and all that will happen to us. This does not mean that we blame the bad things on God. We simply thank God that we know He has our best interests at heart and is doing everything possible to bring them about. We have the assurance that *"all things work together for good"* to us (Romans 8:28). He is worthy of all our praise. He has given us wings and made us heavenly creatures.

All the wings that Ezekiel saw were directed heaven-ward: *Their wings were stretched upward.* None of the wings was partly raised. None of them was half-mast. Not one of the wings was pointed earthward. Every wing was *stretched upward*. Our spirits are to be stretched heavenward in praise and worship. There is no comparison between a miserable-looking bird, crouched down on a rainy day, with its wings folded, and a bird in full flight, with its wings fully extended.

When you stretch your wings upward and learn to praise God, you create a different atmosphere. We call it an "atmosphere of praise". It is actually the very presence of God, His glory. For God dwells in the midst of the praises of His people.

> *But thou art holy, O thou that inhabitest the praises of Israel.*
> Psalms 22:3

Because He loves our praise and dwells in the praises of His people, God has commanded us to praise Him. Many of the Psalms are dedicated to praise. All of the final Psalms — 146 through 150 — are dedicated to praise. Praise is not something that only a select few can and should do. David tells us:

> *Let every thing that hath breath praise the Lord. Praise ye the Lord.*
> Psalms 150:6

Every living creature is capable of praise, so everything that lives and breathes should praise Him. In this way, we create a heavenly atmosphere right here on the earth. We bring down the glory of the presence of the Lord.

Praise ye the Lord. Stretch your wings upward. If all of us would do it together with all our might, there is no telling what we might accomplish.

We simply cannot wait until we feel good to begin to praise God. If we have breath, we are commanded to use it for His glory. Dead people can't praise Him, but the living must.

And two [wings] *covered their bodies:* The Holy Ghost, the presence of God, His glory in our lives, is our covering. Being baptized in the Holy Ghost does not necessarily mean that we are good. Ministering in the Spirit does not necessarily mean we have great spiritual attributes. But when the Holy Ghost comes upon our flesh, He begins to work on our flesh and to make us good — if we allow Him to do it.

God does not baptize us with the Holy Ghost because we are good. He baptizes us with the Holy Ghost to make us good. We are not perfect at that point, we are only beginning the process of perfection.

Isaiah prophesied of the coming of Christ:

> *The Spirit of the Lord God is upon me; because the Lord hath anointed me to preach good tidings unto the meek; he hath sent me to bind up the brokenhearted, to proclaim liberty to the captives, and the opening of the prison to them that are bound; To proclaim the acceptable year of the Lord, and the day of vengeance of our God; to comfort all that mourn; To appoint unto them that mourn in Zion, to give unto them beauty for ashes, the oil of joy for mourning, the garment of praise for the spirit of heaviness; that they might be called trees of righteousness, the planting of the Lord, that he might be glorified. And they shall build the old wastes, they shall raise up the former desolations, and they shall repair the waste cities, the desolations of many generations. And strangers shall stand and feed your flocks, and the sons of the alien shall be your plowmen and your vinedressers. But ye shall be named the Priests of the Lord: men shall call you the Ministers of our God: ye shall eat the riches of the Gentiles, and in their glory shall ye boast yourselves.*
>
> Isaiah 61:1-6

Later, Jesus would quote these words and make them His own: *"The Spirit of the Lord is upon me"* (Luke 4:18). It was the Spirit of the Lord upon Jesus that made Him God's Anointed and that prepared Him to do battle with the Enemy of our souls.

We need the covering of the Spirit. Without it we are naked and defenceless before our enemies. The anointing of the Spirit is a covering which no enemy can penetrate. The two wings that *covered their bodies* portrays the Spirit of the Lord God which is upon us.

You may feel unprotected and vulnerable, but God sees you as protected and covered. Satan cannot touch us unless we allow him to do so. And God will never give him such permission. Never! He will not allow Satan to touch your soul. He will not allow Satan to touch your body. He has no right to do that. You are covered by the Spirit of God.

Like all of God's promises, in order to experience this protection, you must believe it and receive it. When Satan tries to encroach upon you, you must be quick to say to him, "You cannot touch me. I am covered in the Spirit of Jesus. God's protection is on me. You have no right to touch my life." And, unless you weaken and give him permission to do so, he cannot touch you.

Never blame God when things go wrong in your life. Never accept the lie that *God allowed it to happen*. He wants only the very best for you. His will is only the highest for your life. If something has gone wrong in your life, don't look for a way to blame God. Look for your own weakness that has permitted the Enemy to attack you, and ask God to strengthen your faith so that it will not happen again.

Satan has no rights where the child of God is concerned. He is no member of our family. He has no privileges in our houses. Don't give him any space in your life. Believe for the covering wings of the Spirit.

If you doubt the goodness of God in your life and believe that Satan has power over you, you need to repeat out loud the promise of the Lord: *The Spirit of the Lord God is upon me*. Say it several times, and believe it in your heart.

The purpose of the anointing, the covering of the Holy Spirit, is to tear down the strongholds of the Enemy. With this anointing we can *preach good tidings unto the meek*. We are not called to commiserate with the needy. We are called to *preach good tidings*. We are sent to *bind up the brokenhearted*. We are sent to *proclaim liberty to the captives*. Some people would meekly suggest to a prisoner to pray that he might somehow be released. Our challenge, however, is to boldly *proclaim* their *liberty*. We are sent to proclaim *the opening of the prison to them that are bound*.

A lady asked me to pray for her that a condition in her body would be healed. I prayed, and God healed her. Later she said, "I don't think I ever told you that I had migraine headaches for years. Since you prayed, I haven't had another migraine headache." We weren't praying specifically for migraine headaches, but we were proclaiming liberty to the bound, and all her ailments had to go. Satan has no power over us — when the Spirit of God is moving in our lives.

We are called to heal. We know that only God can do that; but, because He is in us, we are healers. Because His power is in us, we are deliverers. We are covered by the wings of God's Spirit.

When Jesus returned to His home town and visited the synagogue, He was given the privilege of reading the biblical text that day. When they handed Him the scroll of Isaiah, He read this glorious passage. When He had finished, He closed the book and sat down. Noticing that every eye was on Him, He said to them:

This day is this scripture fulfilled in your ears.   Luke 4:21

Those present were not pleased with Jesus' words. Feeling that He was blaspheming God, they became very angry and wanted to kill Him. Only a miracle allowed Him to escape. Unseen, He disappeared from their midst. They could not harm Him, for He was covered with the wings of the Spirit. What wonderful protection!

The anger and rejection displayed by the people of Nazareth that day was not an unusual reaction. The world could not understand Jesus, and they cannot understand His power in us. When the Body of Christ begins to experience the power of God as He intended, we will also arouse the hatred and passions of many. They will attempt to do us harm. They will fail, however, for we are covered by the wings of the Spirit of God.

Two wings of every one were joined one to another: The joining of the wings represents our joining in one Spirit, in one mind and in one accord. It was not the heads of the living creatures that were joined, it was the wings. Many denominations have been founded through "a joining of heads"; but God portrays His Body, the Church, with joined wings — one new creation by the Spirit of God.

I am sure that, as humans, we may never totally agree on doctrine. The one thing that will unite us will be the force of God's Spirit in our lives. Differences of opinion will always exist. Still, despite differences, brother and sisters can work together in one Spirit. Because of the work of the Spirit in each of us, we can lay aside doctrinal differences and help each other on this road to Glory. It is time to stop splitting hairs over every doctrinal matter.

I don't mind if you don't think exactly like I do. I don't mind if you disagree with me. Fortunately, we don't have to join our heads. It is nearly impossible. Most of those who have tried failed. But if you and I live like Jesus wants us to live, we have fellowship through His blood. We are joined by the Spirit of God, and He makes us one.

The joining of the wings is not happening in the intellectual realm, but in the spiritual realm. We are one in the Spirit, regardless of our human differences.

> *I Therefore, the prisoner of the Lord, beseech you that ye walk worthy of the vocation wherewith ye are called, With all lowliness and meekness, with longsuffering, forbearing one another in love; Endeavouring to keep the unity of the Spirit in the bond of peace.*
> Ephesians 4:1-3

Regardless of what we may think of another Christian, God demands of us a conscientious effort to *keep the unity of the Spirit.* This is a subject dear to His heart. He wants us to become involved in the process too. Some Christians believe that they are called to go out and debate openly with those who don't agree with them. What a twisted sense of mission! We are not called to fight one another. We are called to *keep the unity of the Spirit.*

Christians were never called to have an argument with someone because that individual did not believe the Bible in the same way as they themselves did. But we do have a calling to *endeavour* (try) *to keep the unity in the Spirit in the bond of peace.* You and I can agree in the Spirit without first agreeing on every point of our personal belief. Our agreement has nothing to do with what I think or what you think. It is based on Him, on Who He is, and on what He does. And when we agree on earth, things get done in the heavens.

> *There is one body, and one Spirit, even as ye are called in one hope of your calling; One Lord, one faith, one baptism, One God and Father of all, who is above all, and through all, and in you all. But unto every one of us is given grace according to the measure of the gift of Christ.*   Ephesians 4:4-7

There are a lot of one's in that passage. Only God can bring about this oneness.

> *Wherefore he saith, When he ascended up on high, he led captivity captive, and gave gifts unto men. (Now that he ascended, what is it but that he also descended first into the lower parts of the earth? He that descended is the same also that ascended up far above all heavens, that he might fill all things.) And he gave some, apostles; and some, prophets; and some, evangelists; and some, pastors and teachers; For the perfecting of the saints, for the work of the ministry, for the edifying of the body of Christ: Till we all come in the unity of the faith, and of the knowledge of the Son of God, unto a perfect man, unto the measure of the stature of the fulness of Christ:*
>
> Ephesians 4:8-13

Some think that the *faith* spoken of in this scripture means *doctrine*. But the Bible doesn't say *doctrine*, it says *faith*. This is *the faith of the Son of God*, and *the knowledge of the Son of God*. You endeavour to *keep the unity of the Spirit* until you come together in *the faith of the Son of God*. How can you believe together and have the same faith as Jesus Christ had, if you can't get together in the Spirit? You must be one in the Spirit, if you are to believe together. That's the unity of *the faith of the Son of God*. When you and I come together, and we agree together in the Spirit, and we don't let it matter what you think or I think concerning certain things, but we believe that Jesus Christ does the impossible, God will do the impossible for us.

We must keep *the unity of the Spirit* until we come to the unity *of the faith of the Son of God*. We agree together, and what we are agreeing for is done in heaven.

And the knowledge of the Son of God ... : We need to have *the knowledge of the Son of God*, the same knowledge; not the same quantity, but the same quality. When I know, without a shadow of a doubt, according to the Word of God, that it is God's will to heal every Christian, because healing is *"the children's bread"* (Matthew 15:26), then I can believe God, because I have *the knowledge of the Son of God*, and I have *the faith of the*

Son of God. And so, we must *endeavour to keep the unity of the Spirit,* until we come to *the unity of the faith* and *the knowledge of the Son of God.*

Even as our physical body works together in unity of purpose, the spiritual Body of Jesus Christ must endeavour to work together in unity of Spirit, that the purposes of God might be fulfilled in every member.

Till we all come in the unity of the faith, and of the knowledge of the Son of God ... : One day, as I was reading this passage, I became aware that it was dealing with *the faith of [Jesus] the Son of God* and *the knowledge of [Jesus] the Son of God.* We have been given five ministries in order that we come to that place in God, where we have that same faith as Jesus had when He walked on earth in human flesh and that same knowledge that He was given as a man. Jesus said:

> *Have faith in God. For verily I say unto you, That whosoever shall say unto this mountain, Be thou removed, and be thou cast into the sea; and shall not doubt in his heart, but shall believe that those things which he saith shall come to pass; he shall have whatsoever he saith.*   Mark 11:22-23

Jesus proved that He had this kind of faith and was encouraging His disciples to unite with Him in His faith.

> *Now there is at Jerusalem by the sheep market a pool, which is called in the Hebrew tongue Bethesda, having five porches. In these lay a great multitude of impotent folk, of blind, halt, withered, waiting for the moving of the water. For an angel went down at a certain season into the pool, and troubled the water: whosoever then first after the troubling of the water stepped in was made whole of whatsoever disease he had. And a certain man was there, which had an infirmity thirty and eight years. When Jesus saw him lie, and knew that he had been now a long time in that case, he saith unto him, Wilt thou be made whole? The impotent man answered him, Sir, I have no man, when the water is troubled, to put me into the pool: but while I am coming, another steppeth down before me. Jesus saith unto him,*

Rise, take up thy bed, and walk. And immediately the man was made whole, and took up his bed, and walked: and on the same day was the sabbath. John 5:2-9

Jesus *knew*. He had the knowledge concerning this certain man, but He also "knew" it was God's will to heal him.

But Jesus answered them, My Father worketh hitherto, and I work. Therefore the Jews sought the more to kill him, because he not only had broken the sabbath, but said also that God was his Father, making himself equal with God. Then answered Jesus and said unto them, Verily, verily, I say unto you, The Son can do nothing of himself, but what he seeth the Father do: for what things soever he doeth, these also doeth the Son likewise. For the Father loveth the Son, and sheweth him all things that himself doeth: and he will shew him greater works than these, that ye may marvel. John 5:17-20

It is through the revelation of His Word that Jesus shares His knowledge with us.

We need to come to *the unity of the faith of Jesus Christ* and to know His knowledge in order to mature and come into *the measure of the stature of the fulness of Christ.* This unity with Christ, believing as He does and knowing as He knows, causes us to know that we, His Body, are one in Him by His Spirit. Our wings are joined. God portrayed us in this way to His prophet, Ezekiel; and we are one.

Because the wings of the living creatures were joined, *the likeness of the four living creatures* was one creation; so also is the Body of Jesus Christ, the Church. It cannot be divided. It is *one.*

For as the body is one, and hath many members, and all the members of that one body, being many, are one body: so also is Christ.
I Corinthians 12:12

We are not told that the Church *will be* one. It *is* one. Through the work of the Spirit, we are one body. The last prayer that we have recorded of Jesus was for our oneness.

As thou hast sent me into the world, even so have I also sent them into the world. And for their sakes I sanctify myself, that they also might be sanctified through the truth. Neither pray I for these alone, but for them also which shall believe on me through their word; That they all may be one; as thou, Father, art in me, and I in thee, that they also may be one in us: that the world may believe that thou hast sent me. And the glory which thou gavest me I have given them; that they may be one, even as we are one: I in them, and thou in me, that they may be made perfect in one; and that the world may know that thou hast sent me, and hast loved them, as thou hast loved me.

John 17:18-23

We are *one* in the Spirit. But Jesus prayed that we would experience our oneness, that our oneness would not remain a potential, but become a reality. We are just as much one as He is one with the Father. We are one in ministry. We are one in worship. We are one in conversation. We are one in deeds. Sometimes the chord seems to be unravelled, but it is holding.

Jesus didn't pray prayers that were impossible. He didn't ask the Father to do things that couldn't be done. If He prayed it, we can have it. Now, our oneness must move out of the realm of the theoretical into the realm of the practical.

We must learn to weep with those who weep, to mourn with those who mourn, to laugh with those who laugh, to be happy for each other's blessings, to rejoice in one another's promotions, to enjoy the goodness that God bestows upon others. Then the prayer of Jesus will be fully answered.

When you don't see eye to eye with other believers, stop to think that *you* might have more to learn yourself. Maybe *you* need to ask the Lord to open *your* understanding so that *you* can see what others are already seeing. Instead of condemning them, get the same revelation of truth. If they are wrong, God will show them. But, whatever you do, don't let insignificant matters like a difference of opinion affect your fellowship with others. God has given us the glory which the Father gave to Him. Don't despise the glory of God in your brothers. The wings are joined. We are *one* in the Spirit.

Satan has worked so hard to divide Pentecostal people over interpretations of biblical texts. Since the Word of God is important to us, this area is very sensitive. But God is not a God of debate and contention. He is a God of unconditional love and fellowship Who has said that He makes us *one*. I would much prefer a person who is going on with God — although I might disagree with him on some minor points of doctrine — than a person who agrees with me on everything but does nothing for God.

One day we will all come to the full truth. In the meantime, each of us sees the Word from his or her own viewpoint and each one has chapter and verse to prove his particular position. What must God think of all this? He must be amused, much as an earthly father might be on hearing his children argue about things of which they know little to date. We only see in part. Maybe each of us sees a different part. Just because someone doesn't see the same part that I see doesn't make them wrong, just different. And being different is not a sin. The wings are joined. We are one.

God is joining Anglicans, Episcopalians, Mennonites, Baptists, Methodists and Pentecostals. He is baptizing Roman Catholics and Greek Orthodox people with the Holy Ghost and making them one with us. We may never agree fully on doctrine, but we can all love and serve the Lord Jesus Christ. We can be one — through the Spirit.

Always remember that the heads of the Living Creatures were not joined, but their wings were. Hallelujah! By our wings, we are one.

You have wings. Spread them and take flight.

Chapter VI

The Feet of the Living Creatures

And their feet were straight feet; and the sole of their feet was like the sole of a calf's foot: and they sparkled like the colour of burnished brass.

Ezekiel 1:7

At a time when Ezekiel was a captive and not able to minister (as God had chosen him and appointed him to do), God met him. The heavens were opened to him, and he saw *visions of God*. What he saw was a picture lesson of the Word of God, much as a Sunday school teacher brings to his pupils. The picture lesson concerned the Body of Jesus Christ and the life of the individual believers.

After Ezekiel saw the faces and the wings of the living creatures, he next saw their feet. That brings us down to earth. Nothing is more important than the way believers walk. When I was first saved and filled with the Holy Ghost, I remember hearing various preachers say, "It does not matter how high you jump — as long as you walk straight when you come down." They were right. When Ezekiel saw the living creatures, their feet were *straight feet*.

The Law was given to Israel to help them walk straight. It was a school-master to bring us to Christ (see Galatians 3:24). But now, because we have Christ, we cannot throw the law out of the Bible and declare that we no longer need the law of God. Being a good Christian requires that we walk straight. Our calling, as Christians, is even higher than the Law. We are called to walk like Jesus, and He walked according to a higher law.

The feet of the living creatures went where the Spirit directed them. They did not deviate from the straight path. *They turned not when they went.*

And they went every one straight forward: whither the spirit was to go, they went; and they turned not when they went. Ezekiel 1:12

Because of the guidance of the Spirit of God in our lives, as Christians, we are not under the Law. But we do walk according to the law. There is a difference. The Spirit leads us in a straight path, and when we walk in the Spirit, we do everything that the Law required.

We are not necessarily ruled by the "don'ts" of life. We are ruled by the "dos" of life. Yet, being ruled by the Spirit, we *don't* fulfil *the lusts of the flesh* (see Romans 13:14). Not everyone who has been touched by the Spirit of God has learned this lesson. Being *moved upon* by the Spirit and *walking* in the spirit are two different things. We must not be content to taste the good things of God. We must go further and live in them. The creatures which Ezekiel saw had *straight feet.* That's the way God sees us.

This I say therefore, and testify in the Lord, that ye henceforth walk not as other Gentiles walk, in the vanity of their mind, Having the understanding darkened, being alienated from the life of God through the ignorance that is in them, because of the blindness of their heart: Who being past feeling have given themselves over unto lasciviousness, to work all uncleanness with greediness. But ye have not so learned Christ; If so be that ye have heard him, and have been taught by him, as the truth is in Jesus: That ye put off concerning

the former conversation the old man, which is corrupt according to the deceitful lusts; And be renewed in the spirit of your mind; And that ye put on the new man, which after God is created in righteousness and true holiness. Wherefore putting away lying, speak every man truth with his neighbour: for we are members one of another.
Ephesians 4:17-25

Liars who become new creatures in Christ have to put away their lying. They must put away 'black' lies, and they must put away 'white' lies. Some lies seem very innocent, but they are not. *Put away lying* and God will work on your behalf.

Be ye angry, and sin not: let not the sun go down upon your wrath:
Ephesians 4:26

It is possible to be angry and still not sin. The secret is to never let that anger stay in you past the setting of the sun. Get rid of it before the day ends.

Neither give place to the devil.   Ephesians 4:27

The devil has no place in you that you do not give him. You are a vessel of God, His temple. You should stay so full of the Spirit of God that there is no room for the devil. Don't leave a place for him to get in.

Let him that stole, steal no more: but rather let him labour, working with his hands the thing which is good, that he may have to give to him that needeth. Let no corrupt communication proceed out of your mouth, but that which is good to the use of edifying, that it may minister grace unto the hearers. And grieve not the holy Spirit of God, whereby ye are sealed unto the day of redemption. Let all bitterness, and wrath, and anger, and clamour, and evil speaking, be put away from you, with all malice: And be ye kind one to another, tenderhearted, forgiving one another, even as God for Christ's sake hath forgiven you.   Ephesians 4:28-32

Don't steal. That was one of the Ten Commandments, and it is still valid today. God won't bless thieves — unless they are willing to leave their thievery.

Use your mouth for blessing, not for cursing. Let it *minister grace unto the hearers.*

> *Be ye therefore followers of God, as dear children; And walk in love, as Christ also hath loved us, and hath given himself for us an offering and a sacrifice to God for a sweetsmelling savour.*
>
> Ephesians 5:1-2

We have straight feet, and we are to walk in love.

The best place to practice this teaching is at home. If you don't have a *straight-feet* testimony at home, it won't be worth much anywhere else. Do not let your temper get the best of you at home. Give no place to the devil at home. You have straight feet at home.

The feet of the living creatures were *like the sole of a calf's foot.* Cows have cloven hooves, so the living creatures had separated feet. That's the way God sees us. We have separated feet and must have a separated walk. It was the *clean* animals that had cloven hooves. We are *clean* people before the Lord and have a separated walk. We are separated from the world and separated unto God. We are separated from sin so that we can be separated unto God.

> *Be ye not unequally yoked together with unbelievers: for what fellowship hath righteousness with unrighteousness? and what communion hath light with darkness? And what concord hath Christ with Belial? or what part hath he that believeth with an infidel? And what agreement hath the temple of God with idols? for ye are the temple of the living God; as God hath said, I will dwell in them, and walk in them; and I will be their God, and they shall be my people. Wherefore come out from among them, and be ye separate, saith the Lord, and touch not the unclean thing; and I will receive you. And will be a Father unto you, and ye shall be my sons and daughters, saith the Lord Almighty.*   2 Corinthians 6:14-18

We have separated feet. We cannot be *unequally yoked* with unbelievers. What does that mean? It means exactly what it says. We should not be yoked together with those who do not believe in Jesus Christ as we do.

A yoke ties two animals together. This is not a simple friendship. You can be friends with the people you work with, but you cannot be yoked to them — if they are not believers. You can be friends with the other students in your school, but you cannot be yoked with them. When unbelieving friends become so close that you are yoked together with them, you will find them dragging you down to their level. It doesn't work.

We are to be friends with unbelievers only so that they may see the light in us. If they see that light and begin to glorify the God that is in us, they will be drawn to the light and their feet will start to get separated too, as they come to know Jesus Christ as Saviour.

When Christians make an alliance with unbelievers which is stronger than mere friendship, they rarely make progress in their Christian lives. Instead of influencing their friends for Christ, their friends influence them for the world. I have seen so many cases over the years.

We are not to be yoked with unbelievers in business. The end result will be tragic.

We are not to be yoked with unbelievers in marriage. If we come to know the Lord after we are already married, the Bible gives us instructions about how to go about winning our mates, but it explicitly forbids single believers from marrying unbelievers. No good can come of it. He has called us to *come out from among them,* not to join ourselves to them.

> *Having therefore these promises, dearly beloved, let us cleanse ourselves from all filthiness of the flesh and spirit, perfecting holiness in the fear of God. Receive us; we have wronged no man, we have corrupted no man, we have defrauded no man.*
>
> 2 Corinthians 7:1-2

There are sins that some Christians think are okay. If they would really think about what they are doing, however, they would soon realize that sin, any sin, is a filthiness of the flesh and is not pleasing to God. Anything that you do which makes you smell rotten, for example, is a *filthiness of the flesh.* Any obscene thought is a *filthiness of the spirit.* Filthy minds and filthy bodies must be purified by the blood of Jesus Christ and by the cleansing work of the Holy Ghost.

Some people may not do many wrong acts, yet they have a filthy spirit. God wants us to cleanse ourselves from a filthy spirit. He cannot walk in us the way He wants to when we have a filthy spirit. He has called us to have straight and separated feet.

Cloven hooves keep animals from sinking down into the mire. Holy feet will keep you from sinking down into the filth of the world. Jesus prayed for us:

> *I pray not that thou shouldest take them out of the world, but that thou shouldest keep them from the evil.* John 17:15

He did not pray for us to be taken out of the world. He prayed that God would keep us from the evil of the world. In answer to that prayer, God has given us separated feet so that we need not sink into the mire of sin.

Some Christians say they can't help the things they are doing — because of the people around them. They need to separate themselves from that crowd, if possible. The salvation of our souls is so much more important than losing a few friends. If we are forced to be around nonbelievers, on our jobs, for example, remember that we have separated feet. We do not need to sink into the mire into which others have fallen.

God has allowed us to be on jobs where sinners work so that we can win them to Christ. He did not pray for us to be separated from our jobs. He prayed that we would be separated from the sin into which others around us are sinking. You can take a stand for God and the right wherever you are.

I promised the Lord that I would testify to my co-workers. I was the only woman in my department (there were eight men), but I told those men how God saved my soul. I told them how He shortened my right leg two inches. Every one of them knew that I was a Christian. They didn't have to guess about what I believed.

Because we worked together for ten years, it was a very close-knit group. We all thought a lot of each other. And, although those men did not believe as I did, they respected me. If they let slip with a swear word, they apologized. If they wanted to say something offensive, they did it out of hearing distance. I didn't have to sink into the mud around me. I could lift the others up onto a different plane. This is what separation does for you.

The feet of the living creatures *sparkled*. They were beautiful. We don't usually think of feet as being beautiful. My daughter-in-law, Helen, is the exception. She always argued with my son and daughter about who had nicer toes. She would say to my daughter, Julie, "You have toes like Hughie's. Look at mine. They're so much nicer." It was two against one. When my grandchildren were born, she was happy to see that they had toes like their mother's.

Most people, however, don't find anything beautiful about their feet. The feet which Ezekiel saw *sparkled like burnished brass*. That shouldn't be surprising. Jesus had beautiful feet, and we are predestined to be like Him.

And in the four and twentieth day of the first month, as I was by the side of the great river, which is Hiddekel; Then I lifted up mine eyes, and looked, and behold a certain man clothed in linen, whose loins were girded with fine gold of Uphaz: His body also was like the Beryl, and his face as the appearance of lightning, and his eyes as lamps of fire, and his arms and his feet like in colour to polished brass, and the voice of his words like the voice of a multitude.

Daniel 10:4-6

The prophet Daniel saw the feet of Jesus *like in colour to polished brass,* the same way Ezekiel saw us. We are His reflection in this world. We are to bear His image in the earth. Let this be the most important prayer of our hearts — to be like Jesus. God will always answer that prayer. Remember, He may not answer other prayers if they interfere with the prayer that we be like Jesus.

At one time I was really very concerned why it was that God did not answer what "I thought" was the number one prayer of my life; but apparently it really wasn't. God knew that the number one prayer of my life was to be like Jesus. I had always wanted to be like Jesus, even before I was saved. So, it really was the number one prayer of my life, but I never thought of it that way.

The number one prayer that was always in my heart and on my prayer list was that God would save my husband's soul and bring him home. One day I was making a cake for my mother's birthday the next day and, in the middle of making it I felt that I just could not stand it any longer, without an answer from God. I thought, "Lord, why don't You bring that precious one of mine home? Why don't You do that which I have prayed? What is it? What's wrong with me?"

In desperation, I left the cake in the mixing bowl, went into the bedroom, and got down on my knees. I have often wondered what I would have done if the Lord hadn't taken pity on me and answered me.

"Lord," I prayed, "I'm not getting up off my knees until You tell me why You don't answer this prayer of mine. I have prayed in faith. I have fasted. I have not given up hope. I have done everything I knew to do for years. Yet, You still do not answer. Why?"

God knew that the cake had to be baked for the next day and that I would not want to miss having a cake for my mother's birthday. So, He didn't make me wait long for the answer. He spoke immediately.

Later, I wrote down His words. They were words to this effect: "Ingrid, it is so that you might be likened unto the One Whom you have always prayed to be likened unto, and that you might have greater faith." That was His reason. I want you to know that I am more like Jesus than I was that night when I got down on my knees, and I'll be more like Jesus when I stand before Him. My faith has increased. I have greater faith because of the goodness of God in not bringing my husband home. My husband knew that the door of our home was always open to him, but God was fulfilling His purposes in my life — to make me more like Him. You probably won't be called on to make that kind of consecration in life, but whatever it takes to be more like

Jesus, it's worth it. Jesus did save my husband's soul on his death bed and took him to His eternal home.

We have beautiful feet. Just as the feet of Jesus are pictured, so are ours: sparkling, beautiful, shining feet.

The walk of the Christian is to be a beautiful walk. Paul said that he could weep because of some Christian's walk. It's amazing how many people testify with their mouths about the Lord and, with their feet, walk in sin. I would say it is better to be quite about Jesus when you are walking in sin yourself. How can you lead someone to the Lord when you are leading a life of sin? That gives people a wrong picture of what it means to be a Christian. It makes them believe that our God doesn't care what we do or how we live, and that's a wrong concept.

Our feet are to be in colour as *polished brass*. Brass depicts judgment in the Scriptures.

> *For if we would judge ourselves, we should not be judged.*
> 1 Corinthians 11:31

Polished (refined) judgment of ourselves will bring forth the beauty of Jesus in our walk as Christians. Heaven is a pure place! Heaven is a glorious place! Heaven is a beautiful place! Can you imagine walking around in heaven with muddy, sinful feet? I can't. If you expect to live there, get your feet cleaned up. Let your feet be as those of Jesus.

John saw His feet. Oh, that I may see His feet as John saw them and see my own feet in the same likeness: *fine brass as if they burned in a furnace.*

> *And I turned to see the voice that spake with me. And being turned, I saw seven golden candlesticks; And in the midst of the seven candlesticks one like unto the Son of man, clothed with a garment down to the foot, and girt about the paps with a golden girdle. His head and his hairs were white like wool, as white as snow; and his eyes were as a flame of fire; And his feet like unto fine brass, as if they burned in a furnace; and his voice as the sound of many waters.*
> Revelation 1:12-15

There was a fire about His feet. That's the secret of the holy walk with God. We need the fire of God around our feet. We need the fire of God in our walk. We need the fire of God to burn up all the sin in our lives. We need the fire of God to burn up all our doubts and fears. We need to get the fire of God's Holy Word ingrained in our beings, so that our walk will be straightened. The fire of God gives us straight feet; and if our feet are straight, they will help us through the trials of life.

On the morning of November 24th, 1966, I woke up to find that Satan had attacked my eyesight during the night. I was seeing double and triple. I was determined to believe God for healing and to continue my work faithfully — as pastor of Faith Temple and in the cash department at Eaton's, as well.

I was working, at that time, on the eighth floor. Cash would come up in the tubes from every department. We would check the bills to make sure they were correct, then make change and send it back through the numbered tube. I was responsible to keep my cash correct. At the end of the day, I had to add it up on the adding machine, and it had to match the sales slips. Jesus became Eaton's cashier through me. There was not one mistake in my cash or bills in those weeks of trial.

What a miracle God did to help me! I simply couldn't see well. I had a hard time not bumping into things or into people. I could not see where the steps were. Everything was double and triple. It was such a strain to work and to walk that my eyes were very tired all the time, and they ached.

After this had continued for a couple of weeks, I became very discouraged and wondered, *How long is this going to last?* Finally, I said, "Lord, I can't go on like this. If I am not better by the time coffee break comes, I am going to take my break and see the optometrist."

By the time coffee break came, I was no better, and I went to the elevator and down to the second floor, determined to see the optometrist for an appointment. But, amazingly, my feet took me right past the optician's counter and into the Employee's Cafeteria. My feet walked according to the Word of God that I preached; my feet walked according to the Word of God that I really believed.

I had given my life; I had given my body to the Lord. For years He had healed my body from various ailments, but in a moment of discouragement, in a moment of testing, I said, "Lord, the only thing I can do now is to resort to that which You will do through man."

But God said, "No, you're walking according to My Word," and I walked right by the optical department and never even thought of it. As I sat in the Employee's Cafeteria with my food, I realized what I had done. I said, "God, it doesn't make any difference how long it takes to receive my miracle. I'll not require signs or give You another ultimatum. I'll walk by faith till You give me my sight."

He did. I preached for weeks in Faith Temple, Tuesday evening and twice on Sunday, by faith. I couldn't see to read my Bible or anything else. When I stood up behind the pulpit I knew that when I opened the Bible to read the Word, God would straighten out the letters for me, and He did. I walked and preached by faith until He gave me my sight. That's the walk that God will lead us into, according to His Word. It is according to the Word that you know that God expects you to walk, the Word that He has given to you, to keep in your very being.

And your feet shod with the preparation of the gospel of peace;
Ephesians 6:15

Part of our equipment that we might be able to stand against the wiles of the devil is to put on our feet, shoes — shoes with the brand name "The Preparation of the Gospel of Peace". *The Twentieth Century New Testament* translates this verse:

And with readiness to serve the Good News of Peace as shoes for your feet.

We must fight the good fight of faith, prepared with the knowledge that Jesus Christ has made peace between God and man through the blood of His cross. The battle against Satan was won by Christ for us; therefore, we have peace and victory in every battle. In order to have feet that will fit the "Preparation of the Gospel of Peace" shoes, we must have straight feet, separated feet, *beautiful* feet.

How beautiful upon the mountains are the feet of him that bringeth good tidings, that publisheth peace; that bringeth good tidings of good, that publisheth salvation; that saith unto Zion, Thy God reigneth!   Isaiah 52:7

How beautiful! The feet of the Christian can take the heights. They can run upon the loftiest mountain. They publish peace and bring good tidings. People that bring good news have beautiful feet.

When you visit the hospital, bring the sick people some good tidings. Let them know that they will live and not die. When you visit your sinner friends, bring them some good tidings. Let them know that Jesus paid the price for their sins and shed His blood to cleanse them wholly.

Once, when I returned from a preaching tour, I learned that a dear old saint was in the hospital. Sister Cook was over eighty. She had loved the study of Ezekiel so much that she would go out in 30 below weather and have to take the bus to church. Nothing ever prevented her from hearing the Word of God.

When I arrived at the hospital, I found a Christian worker preparing Sister Cook to die. He was telling her how wonderful it was to go home to be with the Lord. I wondered what impact this message might have on this dear, faithful member of Faith Temple.

When the other person had gone, she turned to me and said, "Praise the Lord, Sister Ingrid, someone thinks I'm going to die. I have news for them, I am going to live; and I am going to get out of here." Sister Cook knew that it was wonderful to go to be with the Lord, but she also knew that you didn't have to be sick to die and that the Lord wanted to heal her. And He did.

Sick people need good news. They need to know that God reigns, that He is still on the throne. He is not taking a nap at the moment of crisis. He is very much aware of what is happening to those who are suffering. Bearing that message makes your feet beautiful.

Stand fast therefore in the liberty wherewith Christ hath made us free, and be not entangled again with the yoke of bondage.
                                                    Galatians 5:1

Stand there! Don't fall for those crooked paths of the devil. Be firm. You have an important message. Satan is defeated.

For, brethren, ye have been called unto liberty; only use not liberty for an occasion to the flesh, but by love serve one another. For all the law is fulfilled in one word, even in this; Thou shalt love thy neighbour as thyself. But if ye bite and devour one another, take heed that ye be not consumed one of another. This I say then, Walk in the Spirit, and ye shall not fulfil the lust of the flesh.

Galatians 5:13-16

Walk in the Spirit and you will not fulfil *the lust of the flesh.* Any desires of your flesh that could be called *lust* will no longer be fulfilled if you learn to walk in the Spirit. What a wonderful truth!

If we live in the Spirit, let us also walk in the Spirit.

Galatians 5:25

If you are a Christian, act like one! Walk like one. Develop a life like that of Jesus Christ. Let your feet be *straight* feet.

Yea, forty years didst thou sustain them in the wilderness, so that they lacked nothing; their clothes waxed not old, and their feet swelled not. Nehemiah 9:21

If God could look after the natural feet of the children of Israel for forty years (they didn't swell in the hot desert sun), how much more will He look after our feet today. He doesn't love us any less than He loved them. We are not any less His servants than they were. Our promise is not lesser than theirs, but greater.

He will keep the feet of his saints, and the wicked shall be silent in darkness; for by strength shall no man prevail. 1 Samuel 2:9

He will keep your feet. Praise God! You don't need to rely on anyone else. He will keep your feet! He will keep the feet of His saints.

And the God of peace shall bruise Satan under your feet shortly. The grace of our Lord Jesus Christ be with you. Amen.

Romans 16:20

Amy Townsend, one of our precious saints in Faith Temple, said that her pastor in Jamaica used to tell them to keep their feet going or the devil would get them. It's true. Keep your feet going for God, and the devil cannot get them. Keep your feet straight, and you will bruise Satan under your heel. You do not need to be afraid of him. He is afraid of you. You are not under his feet. He is under yours.

When Jesus Christ hung on the cross of Calvary, secured with nails through His feet, *the seed of the woman* bruised Satan's head. Hallelujah!

The feet of our blessed Saviour walked a separated walk while on earth. In death, He bruised Satan under His feet which were separated by spikes that had been driven through them by man.

And the sole of their feet was like the sole of a calf's foot: Your separated walk as a Christ-like one bruises the head of Satan and brings him under your feet. Amen! Through Christ's sacrifice, you are more than conquerors over Satan. You have straight and beautiful feet. Walk worthy of your very high calling in God.   ❈

Chapter VII

The Hands of a Man

And they had the hands of a man under their wings on their four sides ... .
                                                                    Ezekiel 1:8

They had the hands of a man under their wings: In other words, it is by the Spirit of the Living God that we minister. It is not by our own strength or by our own power. What we do must be done by the life of the Spirit. This truth is portrayed by the *hands of a man under their wings.* The wings portray to us the life in the Spirit. So, it is by the Spirit of God, by the anointing of God that we minister.

Many people begin the Christian ministry in this way but do not follow on to know the fullness of the ministry that God has foreordained for them. They don't continue in the Spirit; they don't continue to let God move on them in the Spirit, to anoint them to work by the Spirit; and you can't outrun the Spirit of God in your life and have a successful ministry.

Many people never learn to work in the anointing of the Spirit. They are frustrated because they are trying to do God's work in their fleshly abilities, and it simply doesn't work. They have never learned to walk in the Spirit and let the Spirit of God move on them for ministry.

It is impossible to have a successful ministry without the anointing of the Spirit of God on your life. You must keep your hands under the wings and work by the Spirit of God.

This is the way we must see ourselves now, as four faces. Even as the Christ is portrayed by Luke as the man-face; even as the Christ is portrayed by Matthew as the lion-face, the king-face; even as the Christ is portrayed by John as the eagle-face; even as the Christ is portrayed by Mark as the ox-face, the servant. Under each face there was a wing, and, under each wing, *the hands of a man.* Here we want to see *the hands of the man* under each of the four aspects of the living creature, or each aspect of the Body of Jesus Christ, each aspect of your ministry, because we should portray the Christ in all of these ways.

We, first of all, take note that the gifts of God cannot be bought. It is a spiritual gift; and, in Acts 8:3-25, you can read of Simon, who thought that the gift of God could be bought with money. They cannot be bought with money, and they cannot be bought with good works either. They cannot be bought in any way, they are gifts from God. He *"led captivity captive and gave gifts unto men"* (Ephesians 4:8). This part of Ephesians 4 is talking about a gift ministry, for it goes on to say what God's gifts were to the Church: apostles, prophets, pastors, teachers and evangelists. These are His gifts to the Church.

God gives the ministry that He does through me as a pastor to the Church. It's free of charge. He has given that ministry, and He gives that ministry through me. He gives the ministry of a teacher through me. It's given. I don't have anything that I bought or paid for. I only have that which He has given me, and that which He has given to me is all that I can I give to you.

The Hands Under the Wings of the Man-Face

Afterward he appeared unto the eleven as they sat at meat, and upbraided them with their unbelief and hardness of heart, because they believed not them which had seen him after he was risen. And he said unto them, Go ye into all the world, and preach the gospel to every creature. He that believeth and is baptized shall be saved; but he that believeth not shall be damned. And these signs shall follow them that believe; In my name shall they cast out devils; they shall speak with new tongues; They shall take up serpents; and if they drink any deadly thing, it shall not hurt them; they shall lay hands on the sick, and they shall recover. So then after the Lord had spoken unto them, he was received up into heaven, and sat on the right hand of God. And they went forth, and preached every where, the Lord working with them, and confirming the word with signs following. Amen. Mark 16:14-20

This is the ministry that God said those who believe would have to their generation. This is the man-face. This is the face that we must be ready to show to those with whom we work, to those with whom we have to deal, to those with whom we fellowship, in church and out of church.

These signs shall follow them that believe: This is a ministry to our fellow man.

They shall lay hands on the sick, and they shall recover: Many sinners have recovered because I laid my hands on them and, as far as I know, a lot of them have not been saved yet. It's amazing what God will do when you believe. It shouldn't be this way, but I have actually dealt with sinners that had more faith in my prayers than some saints have. They never doubted one little bit that they would be healed, so God did it.

I remember praying for a man who was suffering from DT's (delirium tremens). He was in a terrible condition. He had been drunk for many days and had fallen into a coal bin the night before and had slept there all night in 30 degree below zero weather. He came to church, hoping to get help; and, right there in the church, began to experience the terrible hallucinations common with DT's. I prayed for him and immediately the DT's left him. Then he said to me, "I'd like you to pray for my back." He had hurt himself very badly in the fall.

I asked him, "Do you believe God will heal your back?"

"I believe God can do anything," he answered.

When I had prayed for his back, he said, "Pray for my knees too."

I prayed for his knees, and God healed them too.

How is that possible? It is possible because I prayed with faith in God, and the man believed that God would heal him. So God did it! Stop limiting God. *These signs shall follow them that believe.*

Some people don't believe that God will heal sinners. I do. Jesus didn't stop to ask the sick about the condition of their soul. He loved them and wanted to set them free from every sickness and every oppression of the enemy. Many of them were saved in the process; but that was not a precondition to healing.

Jesus prayed for multitudes of people at one time, not just for those who were saved. He won many to Himself by healing them. And He is still doing the same thing today.

If people insist on serving the devil, God will not go on healing them over and over. Of course not! But don't limit God. He said, *"These signs shall follow them that believe."* He went on to give specifics: *"In my name shall they cast out devils."* Devils have to leave when we minister in the Name of Jesus.

"They shall speak with new tongues," He said. *"They shall take up serpents; and if they drink any deadly thing, it shall not hurt them."* We don't meet up with as many serpents as the disciples of the first century did; but our ministry to this generation must be a ministry of the signs of our time. We face other dangers.

If you do meet a deadly snake, remember that God is greater than any snake and is able to deliver you. Don't spiritualize this passage. It is real. We may not be in danger of being poisoned as much as the disciples of the first century were; but if it happens, we know that God is able to spare our lives.

In many parts of the world, the water is deadly. It is polluted and filled with dangerous diseases. If God sends us to those places, He will take care of us. That is His promise to *them that believe.*

There have been cases in our time of servants of God being poisoned and living to tell about it. That is not to say that you should go around drinking poisonous things as a proof of your "faith". That is the wrong kind of "faith". That is not the purpose of these signs.

The Hands Under the Wings of the Lion-Face

And now, Lord, behold their threatenings: and grant unto thy serv-
ants, that with all boldness they may speak thy word, By stretching
forth thine hand to heal; and that signs and wonders may be done by
the name of thy holy child Jesus. And when they had prayed, the
place was shaken where they were assembled together; and they were
all filled with the Holy Ghost, and they spake the word of God
with boldness.   Acts 4:29-31

The early church was not daunted by persecution. Despite the fact that the High Priest and the chief priests were doing everything they could to quiet the apostles, the disciples continued to believe God for all that He had promised. When they prayed, they quoted the Scriptural promises.

They recognized that the religious leaders of the time were not persecuting them personally, but were against Christ, Who was in them. The works they were doing were not their own. Christ was working through them.

When Peter and John were on their way up to the Temple and saw the crippled man begging, they said, *"Silver and gold have I none; but such as I have give I thee"* (Acts 3:6). They had nothing of their own to offer. What they had was healing from Christ.

As the people of their day had rejected Christ and persecuted Him, now they were rejecting His disciples and persecuting them. They were determined, however, not to let this hinder their ministry among the people and prayed for more boldness to continue preaching and healing.

They were praying for the lion-face. They recognized that they were mere men; but they knew that if they could put on the lion-face, people would hear them roar as they passed by. How could this be accomplished? The disciples knew: *By stretching forth thine hand to heal; and that signs and wonders may be done by the name of thy holy child Jesus.* The hand of Christ manifested through our hands brings boldness to the Church and its ministers.

God's answer to this prayer of faith was immediate: *the place was shaken where they were assembled together; and they were all filled with the Holy Ghost, and they spake the word of God with boldness.* In order to speak the Word of God effectively and with the boldness of the lion-face, we must be filled with the Holy Ghost. The power of the Holy Ghost produces a healthy fear.

> *And great fear came upon all the church, and upon as many as heard these things.*   Act 5:11

In this instance, the fear the people felt was a result of the boldness of Peter in speaking to Ananias and Sapphira.

> *But a certain man named Ananias, with Sapphira his wife, sold a possession, And kept back part of the price, his wife also being privy to it, and brought a certain part, and laid it at the apostles' feet. But Peter said, Ananias, why hath Satan filled thine heart to lie to the Holy Ghost, and to keep back part of the price of the land? Whiles it remained, was it not thine own? and after it was sold, was it not in thine own power? why hast thou conceived this thing in thine heart? thou hast not lied unto men, but unto God. And Ananias hearing these words fell down, and gave up the ghost: and great fear came on all them that heard these things. And the young men arose, wound him up, and carried him out, and buried him.*   Acts 5:1-6

The land this couple sold was theirs. They were not compelled to sell it. Nobody was requiring that they give the profit of the sale to the Lord's work. If they wanted to, they could give a portion of the profit. It was theirs to give, as they wished. Why did they need to lie about it? Why pretend to be giving all, when they were, in reality, giving only a part? Peter boldly stated the facts of the case.

This was clearly the boldness of the Holy Ghost upon Peter. You cannot do this in yourself, without the anointing of the Spirit. God honoured Peter's words and judged Ananias. He fell down dead.

Three hours later his wife came. Before she could learn what had happened to her husband, Peter asked her to tell him again about the donation of the money from the land sale. He wanted to give her a chance to tell the truth. She insisted, however, that they had given their entire profit.

> *Then Peter said unto her, How is it that ye have agreed together to tempt the Spirit of the Lord? behold, the feet of them which have buried thy husband are at the door, and shall carry thee out.*
>
> Acts 5:9

What Peter did took lion-like boldness. Can you imagine what the carnal Christians must have been saying? "Dear me, listen to Peter. He's killing them instead of bringing them into the fold."

The truth is that Peter's boldness was bringing in people by the thousands. That, however, didn't make it any easier to speak out in such a clear way. To obey God in the difficult things He calls us to do, we need lion-like boldness. Many of the things the Lord says through us are not pleasant things; yet we must obey Him.

God's judgment upon Ananias and Sapphira was not unloving. He had to put seriousness into the Church from the beginning. In that way, thousands were saved from lying and going to hell. Lying is a serious sin.

> *But the fearful, and unbelieving, and abominable, and murderers, and whoremongers, and sorcerers, and idolaters, and all liars, shall have their part in the lake which burneth with fire and brimstone: which is the second death.* Revelation 21:8

God gives us many opportunities to repent. When we refuse to do so, He must exercise judgment — for justice sake, and for the good of all saints. That doesn't, in any way, take away from the goodness and kindness of our God. That is a manifestation of His goodness and kindness.

Discipline is needed in the Church. Few, however, have the boldness to do what they know to be the will of God. Thank God that Peter had that boldness. It resulted in a far greater ministry.

And by the hands of the apostles were many signs and wonders wrought among the people; (and they were all with one accord in Solomon's porch. And of the rest durst no man join himself to them: but the people magnified them. And believers were the more added to the Lord, multitudes both of men and women.)   Acts 5:12-14

From that day, in which God (through Peter) exercised judgment upon Ananias and Sapphira, insincere and half-hearted people did not join themselves to the apostles. They were afraid to do it. This protected the Church from hypocrisy.

We need the balance of the goodness of God and the severity of God in our gospel witness. We must tell people about the necessity to maintain a clean spirit and to lead a clean life. These days, it seems that people are looking to see what they can get by with instead of looking to see how they can please the Lord in their lives. We need more seriousness in the Church so that insincere people will be afraid. This will not hinder the growth of the Church in any way. *And believers were the more added to the Lord, multitudes both of men and women.*

Many people believe that if the Church begins to strictly obey God, nobody will come, and nobody will get saved. The truth is just the opposite. When we get serious with God and start doing His will, that's when sinners are drawn to the church. That's when many people repent and give their hearts to Jesus.

Insomuch that they brought forth the sick into the streets, and laid them on beds and couches, that at the least the shadow of Peter passing by might overshadow some of them.   Acts 5:15

Peter was such a lion-like man that his very shadow was charged with the power of God. When it passed over the sick, they were healed.

There came also a multitude out of the cities round about unto Jerusalem, bringing sick folks, and them which were vexed with unclean spirits: and they were healed every one.   Acts 5:16

We need the ministry of the hands under the wings of the lion-face.

The Hands Under the Wings of the Ox-Face

Now there was at Joppa a certain disciple named Tabitha, which by interpretation is called Dorcas: this woman was full of good works and almsdeeds which she did. And it came to pass in those days, that she was sick, and died: whom when they had washed, they laid her in an upper chamber. And forasmuch as Lydda was nigh to Joppa, and the disciples had heard that Peter was there, they sent unto him two men, desiring him that he would not delay to come to them. Then Peter arose and went with them. When he was come, they brought him into the upper chamber: and all the widows stood by him weeping, and shewing the coats and garments which Dorcas made, while she was with them.   Acts 9:36-39

The funeral arrangements were already made, but nobody was happy about that. Dorcas had made so many good things for the people with her hands that great numbers of people were mourning her passing. She had a servant's heart. We don't have nearly enough people like her today. This is strange, in a way, because the ministry of service to others is just as blessed and just as rewarding as any other ministry in the Body of Jesus Christ. The problem is that we don't see it that way. We prefer the public positions, where we are seen and heard, and, perhaps, more appreciated by others.

Every pastor is eager for more true servants. I am. And Christ is eager for more true servants, as well. He came as a servant Himself. The Enemy of our souls would make us believe that when we help one another we are not accomplishing anything of significance. This is not true. What could be more significant than service?

There are many poor and needy people who are just waiting for the Body of Christ to prove its love and concern in a more tangible way. It requires time, something that few are willing to give. It requires willingness, something that few have. And it requires an effort on your part, something that few are willing to put forth. Yet the rewards are great. Nothing could be more rewarding. And no ministry will win more souls.

These people of the first century could not accept the fact that a person of such loving service would be taken from them. They simply could not go on with the funeral service for Dorcas. They desperately needed this loving and caring person.

Sometimes we think that our ministry is unnoticed and unappreciated. It might be unnoticed and unappreciated by men; but the Lord knows what we are doing; and we will never go unrewarded.

These people had enough faith to call for Peter, but they didn't have enough faith to stop crying. That bothered Peter. The wailing was not helping his faith; so he asked them to leave the room while he prayed. That might have hurt the feelings of some; but it was necessary, and it was the Holy Ghost that gave him the wisdom and the courage to do it. Restoring the life of Dorcas was the important thing. If someone's feelings got hurt in the process, that was regrettable, but necessary. He *put them all forth,* every single one of them.

> *But Peter put them all forth, and kneeled down, and prayed; and turning him to the body said, Tabitha, arise. And she opened her eyes: and when she saw Peter, she sat up.*   Acts 9:40

The spirit of Dorcas was gone. Only her body remained. Yet her spirit heard the words of Peter and hurried back to its house.

> *And he gave her his hand, and lifted her up, and when he had called the saints and widows, presented her alive. And it was known throughout all Joppa; and many believed in the Lord.*
>   Acts 9:41-42

It was the hand of God that raised up Dorcas, but He used Peter, and the hand of the Lord, under the lion-face, to do it. Peter had to give Dorcas his hand, just as he had given his hand to the lame man at the Beautiful Gate. Through this miracle, one of the greatest recorded in the Bible, God showed the importance of the ox-face ministry. Dorcas was needed, so her life was miraculously restored, and, as a result, *many believed in the Lord.*

The Hands Under the Wings of the Eagle-Face

And Moses said unto the people, Fear ye not, stand still, and see the salvation of the Lord, which he will shew to you to day: for the Egyptians whom ye have seen to day, ye shall see them again no more for ever. The Lord shall fight for you, and ye shall hold your peace.   Exodus 14:13-14

Moses was called of God to lead the children of Israel to the Promised Land. When he got to the Red Sea, however, he found that there was nowhere to go. He could not go through the wilderness. He could not go back to Egypt; and how could he go through the sea?

The people were aware of the situation and became very frightened, because the Egyptian army was pursuing them. They were sure they were about to die — after all they had been through. *Perhaps it would have been better never to have left Egypt,* they thought. This made them angry with Moses and distrustful of his leadership. Some decided that Moses should be stoned.

In this moment of confusion and mutiny, Moses cried out to God to do something. He knew that God had been faithful to help them at every step of the way. How could He fail them now?

And the Lord said unto Moses, Wherefore criest thou unto me? speak unto the children of Israel, that they go forward: But lift thou up thy rod, and stretch out thine hand over the sea, and divide it: and the children of Israel shall go on dry ground through the midst of the sea. And I, behold, I will harden the hearts of the Egyptians, and they shall follow them: and I will get me honour upon Pharaoh, and upon all his host, upon his chariots, and upon his horsemen. And the Egyptians shall know that I am the Lord, when I have gotten me honour upon Pharaoh, upon his chariots, and upon his horsemen. And the angel of God, which went before the camp of Israel, removed and went behind them; and the pillar of the cloud went from before their face, and stood behind them: And it came between the camp of the Egyptians and the camp of Israel; and it was

*a cloud and darkness to them, but it gave light by night to these: so
that the one came not near the other all the night.*

Exodus 14:15-20

Stretch out thine hand over the sea and divide it: God was saying, "Use
your hand, Moses, and I'll use Mine. Don't be concerned over the
muddy bottom of the sea. No one will be stuck in the mud. I'm here to
show Pharaoh and the Egyptians that I am Lord."

The Angel of God walked around behind them and, as the pillar of
cloud, stood behind them. He gave light to the Israelites, and, at the
same time, He gave darkness to the Egyptians. Oh! Hallelujah! For us
to act in power, we need Jesus leading us and standing behind us.

*And Moses stretched out his hand over the sea; and the Lord caused
the sea to go back by a strong east wind all that night, and made the
sea dry land, and the waters were divided.*   Exodus 14:21

It was the hand of Moses that was stretched out over the sea, but it
was God's hand that separated the waters. Moses was convinced that
the God who had sent the plagues upon Egypt, softening the heart of
the Pharaoh and causing him to allow the people to go free, could
again do wonders to enable His people to maintain their freedom and
to move on toward the Promised Land.

*And the children of Israel went into the midst of the sea upon the dry
ground: and the waters were a wall unto them on their right hand,
and on their left.*   Exodus 14:22

The Lord actually congealed the water. It stood up as a wall *on their
right hand, and on their left.* What a miracle! As the water congealed, the
Lord walked along with His gigantic hand dryer, His *strong east wind,*
and dried the bottom of the sea. *The hands of the man* of Moses *under the
wings* of the Holy Ghost had brought the hands of God on the scene.

At a strategic moment, the Lord ran out in the midst of the Egyptian
army and began removing one wheel of each chariot. What confusion!
One time, when I was ministering on the Exodus of God's people from
Egypt, I saw Jesus running from one chariot to another, removing one

wheel from a chariot and moving on to the other. I was so excited as I watched I could scarcely continue preaching.

And the Egyptians pursued, and went in after them to the midst of the sea, even all Pharaoh's horses, his chariots, and his horsemen. And it came to pass, that in the morning watch the Lord looked unto the host of the Egyptians through the pillar of fire and of the cloud, and troubled the host of the Egyptians, And took off their chariot wheels, that they drave them heavily: so that the Egyptians said, Let us flee from the face of Israel; for the Lord fighteth for them against the Egyptians. Exodus 14:23-25

The same Lord that separated the sea now took the wheels off the Egyptian chariots. It is amazing how busy the hand of God gets on our behalf — if and when we believe Him. Nothing is impossible — if we can believe. Our hands can do the works of the eagle-face.

The prophet Elijah, under direction of the Spirit of God, challenged four hundred and fifty prophets of Baal to see who was serving the true God. They were to make identical altars, place upon them identical sacrifices, then pray to see which god would answer by fire. The prophets of Baal called on the name of Baal from morning until noon, with no response.

Can you hear Elijah mocking them? They cried aloud from midday until the evening sacrifice, yet there was *neither voice, nor any to answer, nor any that heeded their cry.*

Elijah began to work with his hands, under the direction of the Spirit of God, the hands of this prophet under the ministry of the wings of the living creatures under the eagle-face.

And Elijah said unto all the people, Come near unto me. And all the people came near unto him. And he repaired the altar of the Lord that was broken down. And Elijah took twelve stones, according to the number of the tribes of the sons of Jacob, unto whom the word of the Lord came, saying, Israel shall be thy name: And with the stones he built an altar in the name of the Lord: and he made a trench about the altar, as great as would contain two measures of seed. And he put the wood in order, and cut the bullock in pieces, and laid him on the wood, and said, Fill four barrels with water, and pour it on the burnt sacrifice, and on the wood. And he said, Do it the second time. And they did it the second time. And he said, Do it the third time. And they did it the third time. And the water ran round about the altar; and he filled the trench also with water.   I Kings 18:30-35

Elijah said unto all the people, "Come near unto me." And all the people came near unto Him: Then, Elijah worked with his hands. He repaired the altar of the Lord that was broken down. He took twelve stones and, with them, he built an altar in the name of the Lord. He made a trench about the altar. He put the wood in order and cut the bullock in pieces and laid them on the wood.

Then Elijah said to those who stood by, "Fill four barrels with water, and pour it on the burnt sacrifice, and on the wood."

In a time of three and a half years drought, would we have four barrels of water to waste on God's sacrifice? Yet, how can I expect to get water if I don't give water? Elijah was obeying the power and authority of God. "Do it the second time," he said, "do it the third time." Twelve barrels of water ran round about the altar. Then he filled the trench with water. Then Elijah prayed, and God did, with His hand, that which He alone could do.

And it came to pass at the time of the offering of the evening sacrifice, that Elijah the prophet came near, and said, Lord God of Abraham, Isaac, and of Israel, let it be known this day that thou art God in Israel, and that I am thy servant, and that I have done all these things at thy word. Hear me, O Lord, hear me, that this people may know that thou art the Lord God, and that thou hast turned their heart back again. Then the fire of the Lord fell, and consumed the burnt sacrifice, and the wood, and the stones, and the dust, and licked up the water that was in the trench. And when all the people saw it, they fell on their faces: and they said, The Lord, he is the God; the Lord, he is the God.   I Kings 18:36-39

The fire that burned in a desert bush without consuming it consumed the brunt sacrifice, the wood, the stones, the dust and licked up the water that was in the trench. The God of fire upon Mount Sinai had appeared on Mount Carmel. Hallelujah!

> *And Elijah said unto them, Take the prophets of Baal; let not one of them escape. And they took them: and Elijah brought them down to the brook Kishon, and slew them there.*   I Kings 18:40

Elijah had no police force nor police dogs to back him up; but he was soaring in the realm of the eagles. He had the power and authority of the Holy Ghost. He commanded that all the false prophets be slain; and he didn't leave the work to another. He did it himself. God was preparing him for a greater witness to his world.

> *And Elijah said unto Ahab, Get thee up, eat and drink; for there is a sound of abundance of rain.*   1 Kings 18:41

People that learn to do the works of the eagle-face grow accustomed to confronting the false prophets and the kings of this world.

> *So Ahab went up to eat and to drink. And Elijah went up to the top of Carmel; and he cast himself down upon the earth, and put his face between his knees, And said to his servant, Go up now, look toward the sea. And he went up, and looked, and said, There is nothing. And he said, Go again seven times.*   1 Kings 18:42-43

Elijah's servant said, "There is nothing."

"Go again!" Elijah told him. He knew what he was talking about. He was not bound by earthly circumstances. He was soaring in the heavenly realm. He knew that rain was coming. He had declared it to the king. It would rain. *Go again!*

If it takes *seven times,* do it seven times. Do whatever it takes. Rain is coming. Stop looking at your lacks, and start expecting some rain in your life.

When the servant had gone six times and looked, he still saw nothing. "Go again," he was told. And this time there was a change.

And it came to pass at the seventh time, that he said, Behold, there ariseth a little cloud out of the sea, like a man's hand. And he said, Go up, say unto Ahab, Prepare thy chariot, and get thee down that the rain stop thee not. And it came to pass in the mean while, that the heaven was black with clouds and wind, and there was a great rain. And Ahab rode, and went to Jezreel.   1 Kings 18:44-45

A cloud the size of a man's hand was enough for Elijah. His faith was not hindered by the lack of physical evidence. His faith was evidence enough. He immediately sent word to Ahab to get in his chariot and move swiftly so that the coming rain would not stop him. The servant saw a tiny cloud, but Elijah saw a mighty downpour. It's all in the way you look at things.

On one of my visits to Israel, I had an unusual experience on Mount Carmel. We were eating in a restaurant there when a heavy rain came. The beating of the rain was so powerful upon the windows that, at first, I thought someone was cleaning them with a power washer. The downpour didn't last long. When we came out, the rain had already subsided.

When we got to our bus, our Jewish guide said to us, "You have just seen a miracle." We thought he was joking with us because we were always witnessing to him about the miracles in our lives.

"I mean it," he said. "You have just seen a miracle. It never rains on Mount Carmel between March and October." (We were there in April). "It's practically unheard of. You saw it with your own eyes."

In that moment, I realized that I had witnessed the same kind of downpour that God sent in Elijah's day. We didn't realize how rare an event we were witnessing, until it was all over. Many of us see miracles and don't realize what we are seeing. We need to get our spirits sensitized to the moving of God. Some may see only a small cloud; but if you have the eagle-face, you will see a downpour.

Ahab believed the prophet Elijah, although he was not a godly king. He called for his chariot (with those superb horses) and started down the hill in the direction of Jezreel. He commanded his driver to go as fast as the horses could take them so that they could beat the rain.

And the hand of the Lord was on Elijah; and he girded up his loins, and ran before Ahab to the entrance of Jezreel. 1 Kings 18:46

I can picture Elijah: a hairy, he-man with long hair, wearing a leather cape, as he girded up his loins to run eighteen miles to Jerusalem. The king of Israel felt a mighty wind behind him and turned to see this phenomenon streaking by him — a combination of hair and leather flying past — propelled by the hand of the Lord in the Jet Stream of the Holy Ghost.

Can you picture it: a hairy man in his flowing garments flying down to Jezreel ahead of the fastest horses in all Israel? How do I explain that? I can only say that nothing is impossible to the man or woman who will minister with hands which are under the wings of the eagle-face. The anointed of the Lord can accomplish the impossible.

God is anointing our hands for service. He is anointing us to work *the works of God,* to do the impossible, to present the signs and wonders to our generation that will convince them of the mighty power of our God and will bring them to His feet in repentance and humility.

Nothing is impossible to us in these last days. Believe Him for these *greater works* He has promised. He sees us with hands under our wings. See yourself as He sees you. ✿

Chapter VIII

Jesus Christ in the Midst of the Churches

As for the likeness of the living creatures, their appearance was like burning coals of fire, and like the appearance of lamps: it went up and down among the living creatures; and the fire was bright, and out of the fire went forth lightning. Ezekiel 1:13

Something about this verse confused me for a time. There seems to be a grammatical contradiction here. First the plural *their* is used, then the singular *it*. I asked the Lord to clarify it for me, and He spoke to me from Genesis:

And God said, Let us make man in our image, after our likeness: and let them have dominion over the fish of the sea, and over the fowl of the air, and over the cattle, and over all the earth, and over every creeping thing that creepeth upon the earth. Genesis 1:26

God took some earth in His hands, formed it into a man, breathed into it His own life, and made it a living soul (Genesis 2:7). So man was made in the image of God. I had always believed it, but now it became real to me: the image of God became the image of man. I began looking at people differently.

I noticed that every time God appeared in Scripture, He appeared in the form of a man. I know that God is not a man, that He is a Spirit; but I also know that God is just as real as any other person that I know. I realized that this presence that *went up and down among the living creatures* was none other than God Himself, living in us, Jesus Christ, walking up and down among His people.

As we have seen, John, in the book of Revelation, saw Jesus in very much the same way that Ezekiel saw Him. Ezekiel saw Him as *lamps and burning coals of fire*. John saw Him as *the brightness of the shining sun*. But both saw Him as a man. What John saw frightened him, and he had to be comforted.

> *And when I saw him, I fell at his feet as dead. And he laid his right hand upon me, saying unto me, Fear not; I am the first and the last: I am he that liveth, and was dead; and, behold, I am alive for evermore, Amen; and have the keys of hell and of death. Write the things which thou hast seen, and the things which are, and the things which shall be hereafter;*   Revelation 1:17-19

Ezekiel's experience was very similar:

> *And when I saw it, I fell upon my face, and I heard a voice of one that spake.*   Ezekiel 1:28

This Being looked like a man, but His glory was far greater than that of any living soul.

Daniel also saw the Lord as a man. We are created in the image of God. We are destined to be like Him. And He is in our midst. He is walking up and down among us. He dwells with me and in me. He is "*Christ in us*" (Colossians 1:27).

As for the likeness of the living creatures [Jesus Christ], *their appearance was like the appearance of lamps: Their* (plural) is used here in the same sense as *let us* is used in Genessis 1:26. The verse continues: *it went up and down among the living creatures.*

It (singular) is used, referring to Jesus Christ, even as Paul writes in Colossians 1:16, *"For by him were all things created."*

Because He came to earth as a man, many did not appreciate His words or realize Who it was who was speaking. They even argued with Him.

> *Then certain of the scribes and of the Pharisees answered, saying, Master, we would see a sign from thee. But he answered and said unto them, An evil and adulterous generation seeketh after a sign; and there shall no sign be given to it, but the sign of the prophet Jonas: For as Jonas was three days and three nights in the whale's belly; so shall the Son of man be three days and three nights in the heart of the earth. The men of Nineveh shall rise in judgment with this generation, and shall condemn it: because they repented at the preaching of Jonas; and, behold, a greater than Jonas is here. The queen of the south shall rise up in the judgment with this generation, and shall condemn it: for she came from the uttermost parts of the earth to hear the wisdom of Solomon; and, behold, a greater than Solomon is here.* Matthew 12:38-42

We need to realize Who He is. He is greater than Jonah. He is greater than Solomon. And He is in us. He is walking up and down among His living creation. He is walking up and down among the churches. Just as surely as John saw Him in the midst of the candlesticks, He is in the midst of the churches today.

He appeared as a man to Joshua. Joshua was wondering how to go about that first battle for the conquest of Canaan, how to take that first of many cities for God and His people. It was walled and well protected. While he was pondering these things, a strange man appeared. It was obvious that he was a soldier, prepared for battle. Joshua asked him: *"Art thou for us, or for our adversaries?"* (Joshua 5:13).

The answer startled him: *"as captain of the host of the Lord am I now come"* (Joshua 5:14).

Joshua reacted to this divine appearance in the same way that both Ezekiel and John did. *"And Joshua fell on his face to the earth, and did worship, and said unto him, What saith my lord unto his servant?"*

The answer was: *"Loose thy shoe from off thy foot; for the place whereon thou standest is holy"* (Joshua 5:15).

Joshua obeyed. He was awed by the presence of God.

Should he have been surprised that God was present for this first battle? Should it have surprised him that he didn't have to go into battle alone? God is with us. He is always with us. He will always be with us. He dwells with us and walks with us. He is our Lord. We have nothing to fear.

That soldier was Jesus Himself. That idea bothers some people. "How could He have been with Joshua," they ask, "even before He was born in the manger?" But Jesus didn't come into existence in Mary's womb. He has always existed. He is from eternity to eternity. He is *"the same yesterday, and to day, and for ever"* (Hebrews 13:8). He has always been, and He always will be.

John, in his first letter to the churches, said that He *"was from the beginning"* (1 John 1:1). His life did not begin in Bethlehem's manger; and, although He was not called Jesus until He became flesh and dwelt among us, to me, He has always been Jesus. Some call Him Jehovah, or Elohim, or Adonai. He is Jesus to me.

When Joshua humbled himself before the *Captain of the host of the Lord,* God told him how to fight the battle against Jericho. On the first day they were to walk around the walls of the city in plain view of the enemy, without saying a word. (When I meet Joshua in heaven, I want to ask him what he thought of that battle plan.) They were to repeat the same performance for five more days, placing themselves in the line of fire of the defenders of Jericho. But they were not alone. The Lord's presence was very real to them. They *passed on before* Him.

> *And it came to pass, when Joshua had spoken unto the people, that the seven priests bearing the seven trumpets of rams' horns* **passed on before the Lord,** *and blew with the trumpets: and the ark of the covenant of the Lord followed them.*   Joshua 6:8

What must have been the response of the people when Joshua called them together to relay this unusual battle plan? How many of them were there? Some say as many as 2.5 million. That's a lot of people to have marching around your city in total silence, isn't it?

When the march had ended that first day, they all went quietly back to their tents. That night, I am sure, Joshua breathed a sigh of relief that he hadn't lost a single person in battle. So far, so good!

The next day and the next, the strange scene was played out again. Each time they did their march and returned to camp without losses the children of Israel must have gained confidence. God knew what He was doing. Then, on the seventh day, they were required to march around the city seven times. God's ways are strange, and we must learn simple obedience to them.

By the time they had marched around the walls many times already, the children of Israel were no longer afraid. They saw that God was working for them. It was at the end of thirteen marches that they were to shout. When they did, the earth opened up and swallowed the walls of the ancient city of Jericho. They *"fell down flat"* (Joshua 6:20). The walls did not fall over, they fell *down*. I have been to Jericho and seen those mysterious walls. They have been the subject of much archaeological study.

As the children of Israel were learning to take the territory promised to them, God was present, walking up and down in the midst of them. Even when Israel later sinned and was taken into captivity, God was with them. He appeared to Daniel in exile. He appeared to Ezekiel in exile. He was with Daniel in the lion's den. He was with Shadrach, Meshach and Abednego in the fiery furnace.

When King Nebuchadnezzar looked into the fire, he saw four men. He was sure that his servants had thrown three men in there. So he called them to inquire: *"Did not we cast three men bound into the midst of the fire?"* (Daniel 3:24). They assured him that they had.

> *He answered and said, Lo, I see four men loose, walking in the midst of the fire, and they have no hurt; and the form of the fourth is like the Son of God.*   Daniel 3:25

There had been three; but there were now four. Jesus appeared there *in the likeness of a man.* Should it seem strange that Ezekiel would see *the likeness of a man going up and down* among the living creatures? No! It was not strange at all. God has always walked with His people; He has always dwelt in their midst.

When Jesus commissioned His disciples and sent them out, He went with them and worked with them (see Mark 16:20). And God has never changed. He is still walking among His people. He is with us every day, everywhere. As He walks with us, we are being changed into His image.

> *And the living creatures ran and returned as the appearance of a flash of lightning.*   Ezekiel 1:14

God is fire. Those who have seen Him have seen fire. When Ezekiel saw Him, he saw fire. When John saw Him, he saw fire. Now, the living creatures are running and returning *as the appearance of a flash of lightning.* We become like Him. There can be no sleeping on this job. No lazy people need apply here. We have a great commission. We must run as a flash of lightning.

God needs those who are willing to sacrifice, knowing that they will gain in the end. He has so much fire and so much light; and the person who is willing to pay a price to serve Him will become like Him.

It is such a sacrifice for people in our Western society to read the Word of God and go to church. They have time for everything else. They have time for their job. They have time for their families. They have time to exercise. They have time to catch the network news. (And there is nothing wrong with all that.) But if you want to be like Jesus, you must take time to receive from Him.

He is fire. He is light. He is our Source of power. Lightning proceeds out of Him. Nothing is more powerful than lightning. It strikes with tremendous force. It strikes so quickly and so precisely. This is the potential power that awaits those who are willing to do God's will.

The disciples forsook all to follow Jesus. They sacrificed their own futures, heard His call, and gave Him their time. The rewards for doing that were great. When they went forth, they went forth in His likeness.

> *And when he had called unto him his twelve disciples, he gave them power against unclean spirits, to cast them out, and to heal all manner of sickness and all manner of disease.*
>
> *These twelve Jesus sent forth, and commanded them, saying, Go not into the way of the Gentiles, and into any city of the Samaritans enter ye not: But go rather to the lost sheep of the house of Israel. And as ye go, preach, saying, The kingdom of heaven is at hand. Heal the sick, cleanse the lepers, raise the dead, cast out devils: freely ye have received, freely give.*   Matthew 10:1, and 5-8

This was His commission. Later, He gave it again in more precise terms.

> *Then the eleven disciples went away into Galilee, into a mountain where Jesus had appointed them. And when they saw him, they worshipped him: but some doubted. And Jesus came and spake unto them, saying, All power is given unto me in heaven and in earth. Go ye therefore, and teach all nations, baptizing them in the name of the Father, and of the Son, and of the Holy Ghost: Teaching them to observe all things whatsoever I have commanded you: and, lo, I am with you alway, even unto the end of the world. Amen.*
>
>   Matthew 28:16-20

He has promised to be with us *alway*[s]. He is *the likeness of the living creatures,* walking *up and down* among us. He is the One standing *in the midst of the candlesticks* today. He will *always* be with us, even *unto the end.*

He was with the seventy who were sent forth.

> *After these things the Lord appointed other seventy also, and sent them two and two before his face into every city and place, whither he himself would come. Therefore said he unto them, The harvest truly is great, but the labourers are few: pray ye therefore the Lord of the harvest, that he would send forth labourers into his harvest. Go your ways: behold, I send you forth as lambs among wolves.*
>
>   Luke 10:1-3

As Ezekiel saw the living creatures running and returning as a flash of lightning, we later see the seventy returning from their mission.

> *And the seventy returned again with joy, saying, Lord, even the devils are subject unto us through thy name.*   Luke 10:17

It worked. They had run out to do Christ's commission and were now returning with stories of victory. God was with them and was working through them.

Now, Jesus promised them more power:

> *And he said unto them, I beheld Satan as lightning fall from heaven. Behold, I give unto you power to tread on serpents and scorpions, and over all the power of the enemy: and nothing shall by any means hurt you.*   Luke 10:18-19

When Satan fell *as lightning* from heaven, he just fell as fast as lightning. The power God gives us is far greater than Satan's power, so far greater that we have power *over all the power of the enemy.* The promise of Jesus was: *Nothing shall by any means hurt you.* God is with us. We have nothing to fear.

> *Notwithstanding in this rejoice not, that the spirits are subject unto you; but rather rejoice, because your names are written in heaven.*
>   Luke 10:20

The person who places his own salvation above all else will never become unbalanced. Nothing is more important than our salvation. We have nothing to be proud of, as far as our ministry is concerned. We can do nothing. It is God's fire that makes us powerful. He does the work through us. It is He who saves souls. It is He who heals the sick.

Yet, we must not lose sight of the fact that we are becoming like Him. He originally made us in His image. When that image was marred because of sin, He came in the likeness of sinful flesh that He might *condemn sin in the flesh* and make us a new creation — like unto Himself. We are a heavenly creation.

After Jesus was crucified, two of the disciples were on their way to Emmaus. They were very sad, feeling that the end had come, when, suddenly, Jesus appeared to them.

> *And he said unto them, What manner of communications are these that ye have one to another, as ye walk, and are sad?*   Luke 24:17

God is concerned about any sadness that His people experience. He wants to know why we are sad. He often appears to us in our lowest moments.

The disciples were amazed that this Person did not know the most important news of the day, that Jesus of Nazareth had been crucified. They had looked to Him to become their king and save them from their enemies. Now He was gone.

> *And beginning at Moses and all the prophets, he expounded unto them in all the scriptures the things concerning himself. And they drew nigh unto the village, whither they went: and he made as though he would have gone further.*   Luke 24:27-28

To this point, the disciples had not recognized Jesus. They did not want this Person to leave, however. They were comforted and challenged by His words. They urged Him to spend the night. He agreed. While they were eating together, He revealed Himself to them.

> *And it came to pass, as he sat at meat with them, he took bread, and blessed it, and brake, and gave to them. And their eyes were opened, and they knew him; and he vanished out of their sight. And they said one to another, Did not our heart burn within us, while he talked with us by the way, and while he opened to us the scriptures? And they rose up the same hour, and returned to Jerusalem, and found the eleven gathered together, and them that were with them, Saying, The Lord is risen indeed, and hath appeared to Simon. And they told what things were done in the way, and how he was known of them in breaking of bread.*   Luke 24:30-35

Now they knew that Jesus was indeed alive. The grave could not hold Him. They immediately got up and returned to Jerusalem to tell the other disciples what had happened to them. Together, they discussed these strange events. The doors were shut tightly for fear of the Jews. It was in that moment that Jesus came again:

> *And as they thus spake, Jesus himself stood in the midst of them, and saith unto them, Peace be unto you.*   Luke 24:36

Locked doors could not keep Jesus out. Strong walls could not prevent His entrance. He is with His people. Nothing can change that fact.

> *But they were terrified and affrighted, and supposed that they had seen a spirit. And he said unto them, Why are ye troubled? and why do thoughts arise in your hearts?*   Luke 24:37-38

Jesus is still asking the same question of His people today: "Why are you troubled? What are you worried about? I am with you."

> *Behold my hands and my feet, that it is I myself: handle me, and see; for a spirit hath not flesh and bones, as ye see me have.*
>   Luke 24:39

A *likeness of the living creatures* is walking *up and down* among us. He has a heart like ours. He feels what we feel. He knows what we are thinking. He understands our fears. *Handle me, and see*, He told them. He was very much like a man.

> *And when he had thus spoken, he shewed them his hands and his feet. And while they yet believed not for joy, and wondered, he said unto them, Have ye here any meat?*   Luke 24:40-41

What more could Jesus do to convince them that He was alive? He showed them his nail-pierced hands. He showed them His spiked feet. When they still couldn't quite comprehend it all, He did something very surprising. He changed the subject entirely and asked if there was anything to eat.

> *And they gave him a piece of a broiled fish, and of an honeycomb.*
> *And he took it, and did eat before them.*   Luke 24:42-43

The same God who ate with Moses and the nobles on Mount Sinai ate with His disciples in a locked room in the city of Jerusalem. He was now in His glorified body and did not need natural food, but He had to prove to them that He was flesh and bone. He was not a ghost. He was real, and He was with His people.

Isn't it amazing? God is willing to come down to our level and walk and talk with us. But, when He does, He has to go to such extremes to prove to us that it is really He Himself. He didn't need the fish nor the honey comb. He made it all. He spoke it all into existence. He ate for our benefit, so that we could believe.

He didn't have to show anyone the marks in His hands or feet. His work on the earth was finished. He did that for us, so that we could see His mission to dwell with men. Touch Him and see.

Just as there were marks of suffering on the body of Jesus, there may be some marks of suffering in our lives, as well.

> *Who now rejoice in my sufferings for you, and fill up that which is*
> *behind of the afflictions of Christ in my flesh for his body's sake,*
> *which is the church:*   Colossians 1:24

If there are such scars on us, we should rejoice. Suffering with Christ can only make us more like Him and help us to identify with Him. Those are marks gladly borne. They exist because I chose to walk with Jesus. I am not ashamed of those marks. They are a sign of my willingness to obey His voice.

> *And he said unto them, These are the words which I spake unto you,*
> *while I was yet with you, that all things must be fulfilled, which*
> *were written in the law of Moses, and in the prophets, and in the*

psalms, concerning me. Then opened he their understanding, that
they might understand the scriptures,   Luke 24:44-45

It took the risen Christ to open to the disciples the complete revelation of Himself. It took the risen Christ to give to John his mighty
revelation on the Isle of Patmos. It took the risen Christ, walking
among His people, to show Ezekiel the *visions of God*. And from His fire
we take fire. From His light we take light. He walks as a man, and we
become like Him.

When the disciples asked Jesus: *"Lord, wilt thou at this time restore*
again the kingdom to Israel?" (Acts 1:6), He answered them:

> *... It is not for you to know the times or the seasons, which the Father*
> *hath put in his own power. But ye shall receive power, after that the*
> *Holy Ghost is come upon you: and ye shall be witnesses unto me*
> *both in Jerusalem, and in all Judaea, and in Samaria, and unto the*
> *uttermost part of the earth.*   Acts 1:7-8

And then the heavens opened on the Day of Pentecost, the Holy
Ghost came as the sound of a rushing, mighty wind, and tongues of
fire sat upon each of their heads. The Host Ghost came to be the revealing and operating power of the Head (Christ) through His Body, the
Church. "He came to take things of Mine," Jesus said, "and to reveal
them unto you, that you, in turn, might shew Me to the world."

> *Howbeit when he, the Spirit of truth, is come, he will guide you into*
> *all truth: for he shall not speak of himself; but whatsoever he shall*
> *hear, that shall he speak: and he will shew you things to come. He*
> *shall glorify me: for he shall receive of mine, and shall shew it*
> *unto you.*   John 16:13-14

Their concern was to become His fire, to bear forth His name. As we
have seen, He would accompany them in the fulfilment of His
commission. The Great Commission is also recorded by Mark:

> *And he said unto them, Go ye into all the world, and preach the*
> *gospel to every creature. He that believeth and is baptized shall be*

saved; but he that believeth not shall be damned. And these signs shall follow them that believe; In my name shall they cast out devils; they shall speak with new tongues; They shall take up serpents; and if they drink any deadly thing, it shall not hurt them; they shall lay hands on the sick, and they shall recover. Mark 16:15-18

When they had received this commission, *they went forth*. They went forth as lightning. They went forth with power. They went forth with Jesus.

When Peter and John encountered the lame man at the Gate Beautiful, they brought him healing, just as Jesus had done to multitudes in His own earthly ministry. Many others were healed in the ministry of the disciples. The ministry of Jesus did not end when He went back to heaven. It continued with the disciples because *He* continued with the disciples. Where He is there are miracles; and He is with those who love and serve Him.

Now, it was the voice of Peter that people heard; but it was the touch of Jesus that drew them to the Father. It was the hand of Peter that was laid upon the sick; but, at the same time, they felt the invisible hand of Jesus on them, and they were healed.

He was with them. He was working with them. The signs that followed their ministries were proof of that fact.

In that same way, God is among us today. Although Jesus is sitting at the right hand of God, He is at work in our midst. He is still *the coal of fire*. He is still *the burning lamp*. He is still *walking up and down among the living creatures*. Would to God that more of us knew it; for this is a life-transforming truth.

So then after the Lord had spoken unto them, he was received up into heaven, and sat on the right hand of God. And they went forth, and preached every where, the Lord working with them, and confirming the word with signs following. Amen. Mark 16:19-20

As we act on His Word, we will see the Lord working with us, confirming the Word with signs following — truly the Christ manifesting Himself as He who walks in the midst of His Church.

And as the fire was bright and out of the fire went forth lightning: the Spirit of revelation in the knowledge of Him. It is as we see Jesus by the Holy Ghost that we can go forth *(rush) and return* (to Him) with the results of His commission. God help us to live in the present revelation of the truth of God's Word. Keep *the coal of fire* burning and your eternal lamp shining *as lightning.*   ✸

Chapter IX

The Wheels and Their Work — the Beryl

Now as I beheld the living creatures, behold one wheel upon the earth by the living creatures, with his four faces. The appearance of the wheels and their work was like unto the colour of a beryl: and they four had one likeness: and their appearance and their work was as it were a wheel in the middle of a wheel. When they went, they went upon their four sides: and they turned not when they went. As for their rings, they were so high that they were dreadful; and their rings were full of eyes round about them four.   Ezekiel 1:15-18

In verse twelve we saw the absolute submission of the living creatures to the Spirit of God: *And they went everyone straight forward: whither the spirit was to go, they went: and they turned not when they went.* We are going to realize the reason for this absolute submission as we examine the wheels of Ezekiel's vision.

Now as I beheld the living creatures, behold ... : As Ezekiel saw the living creatures *running and returning as a flash of lightning,* he beheld the wheels. He said, *"Now."* It was in the brightness of this revelation that Ezekiel first saw the wheels. God grant to us that we may see God's wheels in our lives, as well.

The wheels were beside the living creatures upon the earth. There was *the likeness of four living creatures*, and there were four wheels. There is a definite link between the living creatures and the wheels. *Wheel* means *work* or *wrought* and the wheels portray the work of God in our lives or the purpose of God being worked out in our lives. Therefore, the description of the wheels is the description of the Divine will of God in the Body of Jesus Christ.

The wheels *had one likeness*. God has one unchanging purpose for each of us, and that one purpose is to be conformed to the image of Jesus Christ, to be made like Him. Everything He does in us works toward that end while we are in this life.

We have a heavenly calling, but God has purposed to fulfil it in us while on this earth. The *rings* (rims) of the wheels were so high they were awesome, and yet they were beside the living creatures on the earth. The purpose of God for you and me originated in heaven but is being wrought upon the earth so that God will receive the fulfilment of His Divine will in us, when we meet Him in heaven.

Now as I beheld the living creatures, behold one wheel upon the earth by the living creatures, with his four faces: with the man-face, the lion-face, the ox-face and the eagle-face. God's purposes in us are with us in every aspect of Jesus Christ that we are showing forth in our ministry. It is God's will for us to portray Jesus Christ as the Son of Man to our generation. God is working in us after the counsel of His will that we should manifest power and boldness in His name (the lion face), as well as being humble and contrite in spirit as our Master (the ox face). Hallelujah! The purpose of God is that we *"shall mount up with wings as eagles;"* we *"shall run and not be weary;"* and we *"shall walk, and not faint"*. The wheel was not only *by the living creatures*, but also *with his four faces*.

And their appearance and their work was as it were a wheel in the middle of a wheel: Jesus Christ is that *wheel in the middle of the wheel*. It is through Him that the outer wheel works His will in us. *"Christ in you, the hope of glory."*

It is as the spoke of the wheel moves that the rim of the wheel moves and accomplishes the work that the wheel is designed to do. Each wheel was beside each living creature upon the earth. As the living creatures portray the Christ in His ministry, even so the wheels portray His work in His Body.

As for their rings, they were so high that they were dreadful (awesome). The purpose of God in our lives is a very high calling. It is so high that our carnal minds cannot believe it is possible. To think that God could take a person like me and shape me until I become like Christ is beyond our natural comprehension.

> *Brethren, I count not myself to have apprehended: but this one thing I do, forgetting those things which are behind, and reaching forth unto those things which are before, I press toward the mark for the prize of the high calling of God in Christ Jesus.*
>
> Philippians 3:13-14

And their rings were full of eyes round about them four: God not only shows us His will, but actually makes us a partaker of His will. The *rings* were *full of eyes* so that we could see God's purpose in our lives. When Jesus died, He left us a will we call the New Testament. God wrote this will through men for our benefit. It is not a closed or secret will. It is open to anyone who loves the Lord and is willing to suffer for Him. We need to know the contents of the will, for we are the beneficiaries. As we read the New Testament, we should be conscious of the fact that these are the things left to us by Jesus, that He might fulfil His will in us.

> *Blessed be the God and Father of our Lord Jesus Christ, who hath blessed us with all spiritual blessings in heavenly places in Christ: According as he hath chosen us in him before the foundation of the world, that we should be holy and without blame before him in love: Having predestinated us unto the adoption of children by Jesus Christ to himself, according to the good pleasure of his will, To the praise of the glory of his grace, wherein he hath made us accepted in*

the beloved. In whom we have redemption through his blood, the forgiveness of sins, according to the riches of his grace; Wherein he hath abounded toward us in all wisdom and prudence;

Ephesians 1:3-8

Our God is an awesome God!

The Beryl

The appearance of the wheels and their work was like unto the colour of a beryl. The dictionary defines *beryl* as:

A hard mineral that has been used for centuries as a gem stone. They range in length and width from a fraction of an inch to many feet. Single crystals have been found that weigh more than 25 tons.

The substance called *beryl* is a very hard mineral that has been used as a gemstone *for centuries*. God says that the appearance of His purpose in us looks like this particular gemstone. Ezekiel says: *the appearance of the wheels, and their work,* was like *the colour of a beryl.* Therefore, the work of God in our life fulfilling His purpose within us is also like unto *the colour of a beryl,* an hard and enduring gemstone. We must learn to be absolutely *steadfast, unmovable, always abounding in the work of the Lord, as much as we know that our labour is not in vain in the Lord.* As far as God is concerned, His purpose within us is enduring, like a hard mineral, a gemstone that has real depth, beauty and hardness.

Most beryl crystals are yellow-green in colour. Clear transparent crystals of other colours include a dark green emerald, a blue-green aquamarine, a rose morganite, and a yellow-golden beryl. The *appearance of their wheels and their work* was the colour of such a beryl. The appearance of the work of Christ's purposes within us, as we look into these scriptures, is that we become as gemstones. God wants you for His jewel. He has destined you to become His prized possession, His jewel. He is preparing you to rule and reign with Him throughout eternity. You are a *joint heir* with Him.

And if children, then heirs; heirs of God, and joint-heirs with Christ;
if so be that we suffer with him, that we may be also glorified
together.　　　　　　　　　　　　　　　　　Romans 8:17

Do you know what a *joint heir* is? A *joint heir* with you is one that
inherits the same as you do. You do not split things half and half with a
joint heir. If someone leaves you a million dollars in joint heirship with
someone else, you both own a million; you do not own half a million
each. We are actually a partaker of God's will, and He lets us know
what His will is; the wheels are a portrayal of the will of God in our
lives.

Having made known unto us the mystery of his will, according to
his good pleasure which he hath purposed in himself: That in the
dispensation of the fulness of times he might gather together in one
all things in Christ, both which are in heaven, and which are on
earth; even in him: In whom also we have obtained an inheritance,
being predestinated according to the purpose of him who worketh all
things after the counsel of his own will: That we should be to the
praise of his glory, who first trusted in Christ.
　　　　　　　　　　　　　　　　　　　　Ephesians 1:9-12

This is how the wheel of God is working in our lives — that we might
be *the praise of His glory.* He *worketh all things after the counsel of His own*
will. He's *the wheel in the middle of the wheel.* We can rejoice that He has
made us to be a partaker of His will, and that He has *made known unto*
us the mystery of His will. He will make known to us, in a beautiful
fashion, the will of God for every aspect of our lives.

Ye have seen what I did unto the Egyptians, and how I bare you on
eagles' wings, and brought you unto myself. Now therefore, if ye
will obey my voice indeed, and keep my covenant, then ye shall be a
peculiar treasure unto me above all people: for all the earth is mine:
And ye shall be unto me a kingdom of priests, and an holy nation.
These are the words which thou shalt speak unto the children
of Israel.　　　　　　　　　　　　　　　　　Exodus 19:4-6

We are the children of Abraham by faith, and we are also predestined of God to be His *peculiar treasure*. Many Christians don't see themselves as gemstones. They haven't yet caught sight of God's purpose in choosing them.

> *For thou art an holy people unto the Lord thy God: the Lord thy God hath chosen thee to be a special people unto himself, above all people that are upon the face of the earth.*   Deuteronomy 7:6

God has a special purpose for my life. He chose me to be *holy* and *special*. I believe it.

> *For thou didst separate them from among all the people of the earth, to be thine inheritance, as thou spakest by the hand of Moses thy servant, when thou broughtest our fathers out of Egypt, O Lord God.*   1 Kings 8:53

God separated the children of Israel to be His *inheritance*, and He has also separated His adopted children (by Christ Jesus) to be His *inheritance*. We have an inheritance in Jesus Christ, and God has an inheritance in us.

> *That the God of our Lord Jesus Christ, the Father of glory, may give unto you the spirit of wisdom and revelation in the knowledge of him: The eyes of your understanding being enlightened; that ye may know what is the hope of his calling, and what the riches of the glory of his inheritance in the saints, And what is the exceeding greatness of his power to us-ward who believe, according to the working of his mighty power, Which he wrought in Christ, when he raised him from the dead, and set him at his own right hand in the heavenly places,*   Ephesians 1:17-20

Take note of God's working (His wheels in us, *according to the working of His mighty power which He wrought in Christ*. Remember that *wheel* means *work* or *wrought*).

And they shall be mine, saith the Lord of hosts, in that day when I make up my jewels; and I will spare them, as a man spareth his own son that serveth him. Malachi 3:17

While the world is struggling with the concept of "self-worth", God says that we are destined to be His jewels.

I often call my daughter Julia my jewel. She is precious to me. And we are precious to God. We are His jewels. He has vowed to take care of us because we mean so much to Him.

You are not just an ordinary piece of clay, God's handful of earth that will end up in a coffin. You are a jewel, a precious gemstone. Encourage yourself with these promises from God's Word.

Thou shalt also be a crown of glory in the hand of the Lord, and a royal diadem in the hand of thy God. Isaiah 62:3

A crown of glory! A royal diadem! Which of our earthly jewels could compare to the beauty God has placed within His hand to show forth His royal dignity and power?

And the Lord their God shall save them in that day as the flock of his people: for they shall be as the stones of a crown, lifted up as an ensign upon his land. Zechariah 9:16

Saints of God, you are the stones in His crown. God did not create you to be dragged through the mire of this world. You are destined for the heavenlies.

It breaks God's heart when He sees His children defiling their bodies by partaking of the dirty pleasures of the world. He has made us to be His pleasure. He wants to give us the Kingdom. He has designed us as part of His Body and as the temple of the Holy Ghost.

This is also the reason we are to avoid ostentation. The "beauty" of the world can only cheapen us. We are to wear the beauty of Christ. That is enough attraction. Because we are *the seed of Abraham by faith,* because we are born again by the Spirit of God, and because God has ordained us to be gemstones in His crown, many things of the world have no place in us.

> *Wherefore laying aside all malice, and all guile, and hypocrisies, and envies, and all evil speakings, As newborn babes, desire the sincere milk of the word, that ye may grow thereby: If so be ye have tasted that the Lord is gracious. To whom coming, as unto a living stone, disallowed indeed of men, but chosen of God, and precious, Ye also, as lively stones, are built up a spiritual house, an holy priesthood, to offer up spiritual sacrifices, acceptable to God by Jesus Christ. Wherefore also it is contained in the scripture, Behold, I lay in Sion a chief corner stone, elect, precious: and he that believeth on him shall not be confounded. Unto you therefore which believe he is precious: but unto them which be disobedient, the stone which the builders disallowed, the same is made the head of the corner, And a stone of stumbling, and a rock of offence, even to them which stumble at the word, being disobedient: whereunto also they were appointed. But ye are a chosen generation, a royal priesthood, an holy nation, a peculiar people; that ye should shew forth the praises of him who hath called you out of darkness into his marvellous light; Which in time past were not a people, but are now the people of God: which had not obtained mercy, but now have obtained mercy.*
>
> 1 Peter 2:1-10

Have you ever used the expression, "She is such a gem?" or "He is really special"? It is our way of describing a person's character. We would not call anyone who was malicious "a gem". We would not consider a hypocrite "special". When a person speaks evil of anyone or uses language that is not of God, we do not think of them as "a living stone to be desired".

Malice, along with these other characteristics mentioned by Peter, has no place in a beautiful gemstone. Get rid of it. See yourself as God sees you. He is the *living* stone, and has made us *precious* stones, as well. To many of the people of His day, Jesus looked just like any other person. They rejected Him. They refused Him. He was *disallowed indeed of men.* They were blinded to His real worth. But God chose Jesus and knew that He was *precious.*

This is the same dilemma we face in our world today. When we look at each other, sometimes we don't see anything very unusual. We may think some people could never become precious gems. But God is working on all of us. He is cutting away that which is of no value and polishing that which remains to make of us precious stones. He knows that underneath our rough exterior is a *beryl.*

This is our inheritance. Everything Jesus left us is precious and valuable. These blessings cannot be purchased with silver and gold. Only one price was sufficient, that of the blood of Christ. This will was written in His own blood. How is it possible, then, that God's children would desecrate the sanctity of the pure and precious blood of Jesus by partaking of the works of the flesh? How this must distress Him! His plan for us is so high, we simply cannot afford to settle for less than His best.

When you keep passages of sacred Scripture (like this one in I Peter), in your hearts and minds, you will have no room for *malice, guile, hypocrisy* or *envy* there, and your tongue will be separated from all *evil speakings.* Never forget the precious truths concerning your salvation and the purpose of God for your life. Never lose the simplicity of your salvation. Never become so theologically sophisticated that you can no longer appreciate these simple truths and accept God's promises by faith.

> *Wherefore, holy brethren, partakers of the heavenly calling, consider the Apostle and High Priest of our profession, Christ Jesus;*
> Hebrews 3:1

God has made us *partakers of the heavenly calling.* He has determined that nothing is too good for us. We are His gemstones. We are His pride and joy, His jewels. He takes delight in us.

Most beryl crystals are yellow-green. The yellow speaks of divinity, and the green speaks of the earth. We Christians are a mixture of the two. The fact that we have the Christ in us gives us hope that He can change our green, or earthy side. The fact that we do have some green cannot discourage us. The yellow is there; the Divine is present. If we allow God to do it, He will slowly increase the heavenly influence in our lives and decrease the earthly influence.

Some beryls are a very dark green. Right now, I don't see much of Christ in some people; but there is a spark of His life there. They have been born again, and I must believe that God is working in them to change their nature. He hasn't stopped loving them simply because they are imperfect. They are still very precious to Him. He has not changed His will for them. His purpose for their lives remains the same; and one day we will see the results of His matchless grace working in them.

Other beryls are blue-green, the aguamarine stone. The blue speaks of the heavenly. These people have more of the heavenly calling of God manifested in them. They are not entirely separated from the world, but they know what God wants in them and for them. On the one hand, God is calling them up higher in Him; and, on the other hand, the things of the world tug at them. They are precious to God, and He is ever working in them that they may overcome their earthly tendencies and desire more of their heavenly calling manifested in their lives.

A few beryls are rose coloured. That's when people begin to see the Rose of Sharon in us.

> *I am the rose of Sharon, and the lily of the valleys. As the lily among thorns, so is my love among the daughters. As the apple tree among the trees of the wood, so is my beloved among the sons. I sat down under his shadow with great delight, and his fruit was sweet to my taste. He brought me to the banqueting house, and his banner over me was love.*   Song of Solomon 2:1-4

The rose coloured beryl is so beautiful that it has a special name, the rose morganite. God knows us so well. He didn't describe us as diamonds or pearls, but as beryls.

One of our dear old saints who has gone on to be with the Lord was named Rose Cook. To me, she portrayed the rose morganite beryl. Anyone who had the privilege of knowing her will agree. I believe God named her well.

I don't believe anyone becomes a rose beryl in God without first experiencing the Lord in a very special way. Not every Christian can say, *"I sat down under His shadow with great delight, and His fruit was sweet to my taste. He brought me to the banqueting house, and his banner over me was love."*

In order to become a rose beryl in God, we must be taken to His banqueting house and be fed on the riches of His Word.

It takes effort to prepare a good meal, as well as the necessary food items. God, in His wisdom, has given us ministries to feed us:

> *And he gave some, apostles; and some, prophets; and some, evangelists; and some, pastors and teachers; For the perfecting of the saints, for the work of the ministry, for the edifying of the body of Christ: Till we all come in the unity of the faith, and of the knowledge of the Son of God, unto a perfect man, unto the measure of the stature of the fulness of Christ:* Ephesians 4:11-13

Nothing can replace these ministries. Children believe they know best about eating, but we don't allow them to make these decisions because they are too immature. May we allow Jesus to bring us into His banqueting house and feed us on His goodness.

Jesus introduces Himself as *the Rose of Sharon.* In order to be like Him, my Rose Morganite, I must sit down *under His shadow with great delight.* His fruit must be *sweet to my taste.* Then He will bring me to *His banqueting house,* and *His banner over me is love.* Hallelujah!

In January 1949, Rev. J. Styles, from California, laid his hands upon me to receive the gift of prophecy and interpretation of tongues. He then prophesied over me the first prophetic utterance I received from God.

The Lord began speaking by describing the beauty of a rosebud, how it grew, opening its petals to the sunshine and dew of heaven, and the beauty of its fragrance, as it fed upon the fatness of the earth.

Then the Lord continued speaking to me: "Your life is as a rosebud, and you shall become as a full blown Rose fed with the sweetness and fatness of God. And the fragrance of this Rose shall be wafted throughout the world, shedding His fragrance to whomsoever you shall minister."

I was so overcome with the poignancy of God's message to me that I cannot remember other details of the prophecy. I have simply written that which I remember. I am yet awed at His message spoken so long ago. All praise be to the Rose of Sharon, Jesus my King!

I count myself as not having attained, but I press on to fulfil His Word to me. Through the years God has reminded me of this word that He spoke to me; and I thank God that He is still working in me.

He brought me to His banqueting table, and His banner over me was love, that I might eat of His fatness. Oh, to be a rose beryl, to show forth the beauty of the Rose of Sharon, Jesus!

There was also a golden beryl. Daniel saw Christ as the golden beryl.

> *Then I lifted up mine eyes, and looked, and behold a certain man clothed in linen, whose loins were girded with fine gold of Uphaz: His body also was like the Beryl, and his face as the appearance of lightning, and his eyes as lamps of fire, and his arms and his feet like in colour to polished brass, and the voice of his words like the voice of a multitude.*   Daniel 10:5-6

His body was *golden*, His face had the appearance of *lightning* (golden), His eyes were *like lamps of fire* (golden), and His arms and His feet looked *like polished brass* (golden).

The golden beryl is the perfect one. His loins were *girded with fine gold of Uphaz. The fine gold of Uphaz* is a hard and beautiful mineral. Here it symbolizes being girded with the truth of the Word and the anointing of the Holy Ghost. Everything about Him is perfect: His words, His walk, His thoughts.

God has destined us to be a golden beryl, not just yellow-green, not dark green in earthly beauty. Aquamarine stones are beautiful, but let us partake more of the beauty of Jesus and become as the Rose Morganite crystal and, finally, be conformed to His likeness as the Golden Beryl.

> *Behold, what manner of love the Father hath bestowed upon us, that we should be called the sons of God: therefore the world knoweth us*

not, because it knew him not. Beloved, now are we the sons of God, and it doth not yet appear what we shall be: but we know that, when he shall appear, we shall be like him; for we shall see him as he is. And every man that hath this hope in him purifieth himself, even as he is pure. 1 John 3:1-3

As we have read, if you have the hope of becoming like Him, you work toward purifying yourself. If you are not doing that, you need a renewal of hope.

Herein is our love made perfect, that we may have boldness in the day of judgment: because as he is, so are we in this world.
1 John 4:17

God says *in this world,* not in heaven. God sees us as gemstones *in this world.* He pictures us taking on His likeness, as He walks among us in the Church — just as John saw Him *in the midst of the candlesticks.* We don't have to wait until we get to heaven to start putting on the heavenly. We need to start thinking like Christ, seeing things as He sees them, acting like Christ, and talking like Christ. This is what it means to be a true Christian. If we have hope of the eternal, that is reason to work toward perfection NOW. It is time to put on the heavenly and become like the golden beryl.

Beryls are of many different sizes, just as the stature of Christ varies in Christians. We do not, however, have the right to measure ourselves or our spirituality by one another. Christ is our only measuring rod. We are predestined to be made in the fulness of His stature. Let us believe God to do that work in us NOW. God works His purposes in us as we meet His conditions (as we allow the wheels of God to stay beside us on the earth). I have now ministered in over forty countries. The "rosebud" has opened up to some degree (not "a full-blown Rose" as yet), but His fragrance has been wafted on all five continents, and many have come to know the Rose of Sharon through my ministry.

I want to challenge you to allow the Lord to change you into that beautiful rose beryl and to make you like the golden beryl, complete and perfect. May the purpose of God work in your life, so that inside and outside, you will be like Jesus. He is our standard of measurement.

Lord Jesus,

I pray that I shall stand before You in the measure of the fulness of Your stature.

Amen!

Chapter X

The Movement of the Living Creatures and Their Source of Life

And when the living creatures went, the wheels went by them: and when the living creatures were lifted up from the earth, the wheels were lifted up. Whithersoever the spirit was to go, they went, thither was their spirit to go; and the wheels were lifted up over against them: for the spirit of the living creature was in the wheels. When those went, these went; and when those stood, these stood; and when those were lifted up from the earth, the wheels were lifted up over against them: for the spirit of the living creature was in the wheels.

Ezekiel 1:19-21

God, our Creator, is the Source of life in our movements in our mother's womb and throughout life. What we do with that life depends upon us. God, our Redeemer, is the Source of our spiritual life when we are born again and become a member of the Body of Jesus Christ.

Blessed be the God and Father of our Lord Jesus Christ, who hath blessed us with all spiritual blessings in heavenly places in Christ: According as he hath chosen us in him before the foundation of the world, that we should be holy and without blame before him in love: Having predestinated us unto the adoption of children by Jesus Christ to himself, according to the good pleasure of his will, To the praise of the glory of his grace, wherein he hath made us accepted in the beloved. In whom we have redemption through his blood, the forgiveness of sins, according to the riches of his grace;

Ephesians 1:3-7

No person is born into this world by his or her own will. We cannot say that it was by the will of our parents we were given life, for the male sperm has many seeds, but only one unites with the female to give life. God chose us, *in Him, before the foundation of the world that we should be holy and without blame before Him in love.* The wheel of God was working to make us what He had foreordained us to be, before He created the world — a truth incomprehensible to the human mind.

In whom also we have obtained an inheritance, being predestinated according to the purpose of him who worketh all things after the counsel of his own will: That we should be to the praise of his glory, who first trusted in Christ.

Ephesians 1:11-12

The living creatures portray the Body of Jesus Christ. Ezekiel said, concerning the living creatures: *Whithersoever the spirit was to go, they went, thither as their spirits go.* It is imperative that our spirit move with God's Spirit in order to have the ultimate of God's life moving in and through us.

And what is the exceeding greatness of his power to us-ward who believe, according to the working of his mighty power,

Ephesians 1:19

God's purposes *(wheels)* are over, *against,* us when we are walking in God, doing our everyday tasks upon the earth, and also when God's work in us requires that His power be exercised in the heavenlies.

> *For though we walk in the flesh, we do not war after the flesh: (For the weapons of our warfare are not carnal, but mighty through God to the pulling down of strong holds;) Casting down imaginations, and every high thing that exalteth itself against the knowledge of God, and bringing into captivity every thought to the obedience of Christ; And having in a readiness to revenge all disobedience, when your obedience is fulfilled.* 2 Corinthians 10:3-6

This lets us know that our lives, our ministries, have their source in the purposes of God for us.

Whithersoever the spirit was to go, they [the living creatures] *went, thither was their spirit to go; and the wheels were lifted up over against them: for the spirit* [life] *of the living creature was in the wheels.* God has a purpose in giving life to every human being. My life is dependent upon *the wheel* (purpose, work) of God in me. Your life (spirit) has its source in God's work *(wheel)* in your life. In other words, the motivating power of the living creatures was in *the wheels.*

Any vehicle must have wheels in order to move. Then, there must be power to move the wheels of the vehicle, or the vehicle will remain motionless. God has given us His vehicle, the power of the Holy Ghost, in order that His work might be performed in us and through us. It is God's *wheel* or work in our lives that is the motivating power that causes us to move and to do His will.

Paul said to the Philippians:

> *I can do all things through Christ which strengtheneth me.*
> Philippians 4:13

The motivating power of the living creatures was in *the wheels.*

Paul said to the Romans:

What shall we then say to these things? If God be for us, who can be against us? He that spared not his own Son, but delivered him up for us all, how shall he not with him also freely give us all things?
                                                                    Romans 8:31-32

When those [the living creatures] *went, these* [the wheels] *went; and when those* [the living creatures] *stood, these* [the wheels] *stood; and when those* [the living creatures] *were lifted up from the earth, the wheels were lifted up over against them: for* [because] *the spirit of the living creature was in the wheels.*   Ezekiel 1:21

Yes! God works with His present-day living creatures, the Body of Jesus Christ.

And we know that all things work together for good to them that love God, to them who are the called according to his purpose. For whom he did foreknow, he also did predestinate to be conformed to the image of his Son, that he might be the firstborn among many brethren. Moreover whom he did predestinate, them he also called: and whom he called, them he also justified: and whom he justified, them he also glorified.   Romans 8:28-30

And, furthermore, we are God's workmanship. Jesus Christ is the One who gave us life, and our life is in His purposes in us; for He is the One who works in us to make us according to His will.

But God, who is rich in mercy, for his great love wherewith he loved us, Even when we were dead in sins, hath quickened us together with Christ, (by grace ye are saved;) And hath raised us up together, and made us sit together in heavenly places in Christ Jesus: That in the ages to come he might shew the exceeding riches of his grace in his kindness toward us through Christ Jesus. For by grace are ye saved through faith; and that not of yourselves: it is the gift of God: Not of works, lest any man should boast. For we are his workman-ship, created in Christ Jesus unto good works, which God hath before ordained that we should walk in them.   Ephesians 2:4-10

Truly, Jesus Christ was *lifted above all principality and power*, as God raised Him from the dead and *set Him at His own right hand in heavenly places;* and He has *raised us up together in heavenly places* that we might experience His resurrection and translation power in and through us. When we were born again, we experienced a resurrection from spiritual death to spiritual life. No longer is our destination hell after this life, but our destination is heaven, a spiritual place, a place of life and light. In this present, life as a living creature (a new creation), we have the same translation power that raised Jesus from the earth into heaven.

> *But ye shall receive power, after that the Holy Ghost is come upon you: and ye shall be witnesses unto me both in Jerusalem, and in all Judaea, and in Samaria, and unto the uttermost part of the earth. And when he had spoken these things, while they beheld, he was taken up; and a cloud received him out of their sight.*   Acts 1:8-9

This translation power of the Holy Ghost will change the mortal into immortality when Jesus comes back to the earth for His Church, but we have this power in us NOW.

> *For this cause we also, since the day we heard it, do not cease to pray for you, and to desire that ye might be filled with the knowledge of his will in all wisdom and spiritual understanding; That ye might walk worthy of the Lord unto all pleasing, being fruitful in every good work, and increasing in the knowledge of God; Strengthened with all might, according to his glorious power, unto all patience and longsuffering with joyfulness; Giving thanks unto the Father, which hath made us meet to be partakers of the inheritance of the saints in light: Who hath delivered us from the power of darkness, and hath translated us into the kingdom of his dear Son: In whom we have redemption through his blood, even the forgiveness of sins: Who is the image of the invisible God, the firstborn of every creature:*
> Colossians 1:9-15

God has delivered us from *the power of darkness* and has already *translated us into the Kingdom of His dear Son.* This purpose *(wheel)* of God constitutes our life as a Christian (a *living creature*).

In seeing the living creatures lifted up from the earth, Ezekiel was able to see *the likeness of the firmament upon the heads of the living creatures.* He not only saw the heavenly realm but he also saw the ministry of the living creature in the heavenlies. It is so very important that we experience the translation power of the Holy Ghost in our lives and in our ministries. God help us to see the firmament above us today — the signs of our times.

The living creatures went, stood, and were lifted up from the earth; and in every facet of their ministry, *the wheels were over against them.* Whether we are moving in God upon the earth, resting in God (standing) or being lifted up in heavenly places' ministry, God is working in and through us to do His will because we are His workmanship.

The prophet Ezekiel not only became a partaker of the vision that he saw, by eating the Word which God gave him to eat, but Ezekiel experienced the Word which he saw.

And he said unto me, Son of man, stand upon thy feet, and I will speak unto thee. And the spirit entered into me when he spake unto me, and set me upon my feet, that I heard him that spake unto me. And he said unto me, Son of man, I send thee to the children of Israel, to a rebellious nation that hath rebelled against me: they and their fathers have transgressed against me, even unto this very day. But thou, son of man, hear what I say unto thee; Be not thou rebellious like that rebellious house: open thy mouth, and eat that I give thee.   Ezekiel 2:1-3 & 8

Behold, I have made thy face strong against their faces, and thy forehead strong against their foreheads. As an adamant harder than flint have I made thy forehead: fear them not, neither be dismayed at their looks, though they be a rebellious house. Moreover he said unto me, Son of man, all my words that I shall speak unto thee receive in thine heart, and hear with thine ears. And go, get thee to them of the captivity, unto the children of thy people, and speak unto them, and tell them, Thus saith the Lord God; whether they will hear, or whether they will forbear. Then the spirit took me up, and I heard behind me a voice of a great rushing, saying, Blessed be the glory of the Lord from his place. I heard also the noise of the wings of the living creatures that touched one another, and the noise of the wheels over against them, and a noise of a great rushing. So the spirit lifted me up, and took me away, and I went in bitterness, in the heat of my spirit; but the hand of the Lord was strong upon me. Then I came to them of the captivity at Telabib, that dwelt by the river of Chebar, and I sat where they sat, and remained there astonished among them seven days.   Ezekiel 3:8-15

God's purpose in sharing the revelation of the living creatures with Ezekiel was that Ezekiel, His priest, might become Ezekiel, His prophet. And God's purpose in sharing this same revelation with you and me is that we too might come to the fulness of His ministry through us.

Look with me now at the life and ministry of Moses. God engineered every detail of Moses' life, from his birth until his death.

By faith Moses, when he was born, was hid three months of his parents, because they saw he was a proper child; and they were not afraid of the king's commandment. By faith Moses, when he was come to years, refused to be called the son of Pharaoh's daughter; Choosing rather to suffer affliction with the people of God, than to enjoy the pleasures of sin for a season; Esteeming the reproach of Christ greater riches than the treasures in Egypt: for he had respect unto the recompence of the reward. By faith he forsook Egypt, not fearing the wrath of the king: for he endured, as seeing him who is invisible.   Hebrews 11:23-27

These few verses tell about Moses *going* in God's will for the first forty years of his life. (When Moses went, *the wheels* went by him.) We then find Moses *standing* in the will of God for the next forty years of his life.

Now when Pharaoh heard this thing, he sought to slay Moses. But Moses fled from the face of Pharaoh, and dwelt in the land of Midian: and he sat down by a well.   Exodus 2:15

Take note that Moses did not fear Pharaoh (see Hebrews 11:27). He fled in the will of God and was waiting in God's will for the time when God would bring his experience to fulness. When Moses stood in the backside of the desert, *the wheels* (purposes of God) stood by him.

> *Now Moses kept the flock of Jethro his father in law, the priest of Midian: and he led the flock to the backside of the desert, and came to the mountain of God, even to Horeb. And the angel of the Lord appeared unto him in a flame of fire out of the midst of a bush: and he looked, and, behold, the bush burned with fire, and the bush was not consumed. And Moses said, I will now turn aside, and see this great sight, why the bush is not burnt. And when the Lord saw that he turned aside to see, God called unto him out of the midst of the bush, and said, Moses, Moses. And he said, Here am I. And he said, Draw not nigh hither: put off thy shoes from off thy feet, for the place whereon thou standest is holy ground. Moreover he said, I am the God of thy father, the God of Abraham, the God of Isaac, and the God of Jacob. And Moses hid his face; for he was afraid to look upon God. And the Lord said, I have surely seen the affliction of my people which are in Egypt, and have heard their cry by reason of their taskmasters; for I know their sorrows;*   Exodus 3:1-7

Moses' obedience to the call of God was the beginning of being *lifted up* to perform God's will fully in the ministry He had predestined Moses to accomplish.

> *Come now therefore, and I will send thee unto Pharaoh, that thou mayest bring forth my people the children of Israel out of Egypt. And Moses said unto God, Who am I, that I should go unto Pharaoh, and that I should bring forth the children of Israel out of Egypt? And he said, Certainly I will be with thee; and this shall be a token unto thee, that I have sent thee: When thou hast brought forth the people out of Egypt, ye shall serve God upon this mountain.*
>   Exodus 3:10-12

And when Moses was lifted up from the earth in his heavenly calling, *the wheels were lifted up over against him;* for the spirit (the life, the ability to fulfil his call) was in *the wheels* (the purpose of God in sending Moses to bring forth the children of Israel out of Egypt, that the coming Messiah might be born of this redeemed nation in Bethlehem).

Moses' life was lifted up in God for the next forty years; and the purposes of God were always with Moses to perform that which God alone could do.

> *Through faith he kept the passover, and the sprinkling of blood, lest he that destroyed the firstborn should touch them. By faith they passed through the Red sea as by dry land: which the Egyptians assaying to do were drowned.*   Hebrews 11:28-29

The nine plagues could not persuade Pharaoh to let the people go; but when Moses kept the Passover at the command of God, Pharaoh said, "You can go now". Hallelujah! The Red Sea could not stop the children of Israel; for Moses was already *lifted up* to perform the will of God.

For the rest of his life, Moses saw the impossible wrought by The Great I AM. Moses was *lifted up* to Mount Sinai to receive the commandments and ordinances, which are with us to this day. He saw God provide food and water for every one of His people that He had delivered from bondage.

But there was a greater *lifting up from the earth* when the Lord called Moses up to Mount Nebo.

> *And Moses went up from the plains of Moab unto the mountain of Nebo, to the top of Pisgah, that is over against Jericho. And the Lord shewed him all the land of Gilead, unto Dan, And all Naphtali, and the land of Ephraim, and Manasseh, and all the land of Judah, unto the utmost sea, And the south, and the plain of the valley of Jericho, the city of palm trees, unto Zoar. And the Lord said unto him, This is the land which I sware unto Abraham, unto Isaac, and unto Jacob, saying, I will give it unto thy seed: I have caused thee to see it with thine eyes, but thou shalt not go over thither. So Moses the servant of the Lord died there in the land of Moab, according to the word of the Lord. And he buried him in a valley in the land of Moab, over*

against Bethpeor: but no man knoweth of his sepulchre unto this day. And Moses was an hundred and twenty years old when he died: his eye was not dim, nor his natural force abated.

Deuteronomy 34:1-7

Moses was *lifted up from the earth* that God might have him forever with Himself.

We must not forget to mention the *visit* that Moses made to his promised land. He and Elijah visited with Jesus on a high mountain. Jesus, the One who had appear to Moses in the burning bush, the One with whom Moses had been for eighty days and nights on Mount Sinai, the One who had led him all of his life — on the Nile River, in the palace, in the desert, and in leading the children of Israel out of Egypt — now stood before Moses in the flesh, but transfigured by the Glory of God. And Moses had the privilege of telling The Great I AM that it is not difficult to yield your life into the hands of the Immortal God that has been with you throughout your life.

May we each know the joy of being in the perfect will of God through life, so that we may experience the satisfaction of ministering to that Great I AM, not only in this life, but in the life to come, ministering to Jesus in His glory throughout eternity!   ✴

Chapter XI

Terrible Crystal

And the likeness of the firmament upon the heads of the living creature was as the colour of the terrible crystal, stretched forth over their heads above. And under the firmament were their wings straight, the one toward the other: every one had two, which covered on this side, and every one had two, which covered on that side, their bodies. And when they went, I heard the noise of their wings, like the noise of great waters, as the voice of the almighty, the voice of speech, as the noise of an host: when they stood, they let down their wings.
Ezekiel 1:22-24

The word *firmament* means *an expansion* and is used to refer to *the heavens, the vault of heaven, or the sky*. The sky over the heads of the living creatures was *the colour of terrible crystal*. What does that mean?

Something *terrible* causes fear. It is *dreadful, distressing, severe* or *awful*. It is *frightful, appalling, horrible,* or *shocking*. What exactly did Ezekiel see in the heavens above our heads? I believe he saw the purity of the saints of God coming forth in a dreadful and shocking period of time.

But under the firmament Ezekiel saw the wings of the living creatures in perfect formation, *straight, the one toward the other,* ready to
march as an army.

Two of the four wings of the living creatures covered their bodies,
giving them complete protection.

> *Thus were their faces: and their wings were stretched upward; two*
> *wings of every one were joined one to another, and two covered their*
> *bodies. And they went every one straight forward: whither the spirit*
> *was to go, they went; and they turned not when they went.*
>
> Ezekiel 1:11-12

And when they went, I heard ... : Ezekiel not only saw this mighty host
but he heard the sound of the army of the Lord: *the noise of their wings*
like the noise of great waters. Their praise, as they marched, sounded like
the praise in heaven.

> *And a voice came out of the throne, saying, Praise our God, all ye his*
> *servants, and ye that fear him, both small and great. And I heard as*
> *it were the voice of a great multitude, and as the voice of many*
> *waters, and as the voice of mighty thunderings, saying, Alleluia: for*
> *the Lord God omnipotent reigneth.*   Revelation 19:5-6

As the voice of the Almighty: The army had the prophetic voice of God,
ordering the strategy of the warfare. Remember how God ordered
King Jehoshaphat's army through His prophet Jahaziel?

> *Ye shall not need to fight in this battle: set yourselves, stand ye still,*
> *and see the salvation of the Lord with you, O Judah and Jerusalem:*
> *fear not, nor be dismayed; to morrow go out against them: for the*
> *Lord will be with you. And Jehoshaphat bowed his head with his face*
> *to the ground: and all Judah and the inhabitants of Jerusalem fell*
> *before the Lord, worshipping the Lord. And the Levites, of the chil-*
> *dren of the Kohathites, and of the children of the Korhites, stood up*
> *to praise the Lord God of Israel with a loud voice on high. And they*
> *rose early in the morning, and went forth into the wilderness of*

Tekoa: and as they went forth, Jehoshaphat stood and said, Hear me, O Judah, and ye inhabitants of Jerusalem; Believe in the Lord your God, so shall ye be established; believe his prophets, so shall ye prosper. And when he had consulted with the people, he appointed singers unto the Lord, and that should praise the beauty of holiness, as they went out before the army, and to say, Praise the Lord; for his mercy endureth for ever. And when they began to sing and to praise, the Lord set ambushments against the children of Ammon, Moab, and mount Seir, which were come against Judah; and they were smitten. II Chronicles 20:17-22

And when they began to sing and to praise, the Lord set ambushments against the enemy: How necessary it is to have the voice of God through the prophet and through the gift of prophecy in the Church today! Stretched over the heads of the living creature was *the likeness of the firmament* (the expanse of heaven) *as the colour of terrible crystal.*

Crystal expands. The whole process of crystallization is amazing. According to *The World Book*:

Living things, such as dandelions and dogs, grow from tiny seeds or eggs to a form which distinguishes them from other living things. Most non-living substances, such as table salt, sugar or ice can also grow from a very small beginning into definite shapes. These shapes consist of smooth, flat surfaces that meet in sharp edges or corners, and the process by which non-living substances grow into bodies of such shapes is called crystallization.

If you have ever been into underground caves, you have probably seen this process at work. Water, containing dissolved minerals, drips through into the caves in certain points and leaves deposits of those minerals. The amazing thing is that it happens by the simple action of a single drop of water (repeated over and over again).

The dripping of the water over long periods creates very beautiful and unique forms. In caves which are frequented by tourists, these form are given interesting names, depending on what they look like.

One of those I have seen in the caves in the Black Hills is called "the Madonna and Child". You can actually see the outline of Mary and the Child Jesus in that crystallized form.

What an amazing process!

The point is that God is able to form something amazing from materials that look nothing like the final product. Would you ever look at a dandelion seed and imagine that it could produce a dandelion? Probably not. If you didn't know it, would you imagine that milk could make a baby grow? Probably not. God has created some amazing processes.

You don't consist of milk, do you? And yet it was milk that made you grow as a baby. You're not an egg are you? And yet you eat eggs, and they make you grow. You're not a vegetable; and yet you eat vegetables, and they cause you to grow. Your growth is from substances that are very different from yourself. It is the same with cattle and the same with birds. A bird isn't a worm, but a bird grows by eating worms. How great our God is!

For non-living substances, the method for expansion is this slow layer-by-layer buildup that produces something truly amazing. God is working to produce in you a gem of great value. Let Him do His work.

Crystals form by adding layer upon layer of their own substance. This takes time. God's purpose in us is that we grow, adding layer upon layer, to finally become like Jesus. It doesn't happen all at once. Little by little, layer upon layer, He is formed in us.

> *Wherefore gird up the loins of your mind, be sober, and hope to the end for the grace that is to be brought unto you at the revelation of Jesus Christ;*   1 Peter 1:13

In other words, take hold of your mind. Students do it when they cram for an examination. They *gird up the loins* of their mind. They want to get a good mark, so they get serious. They get hold of their mind and prepare for the test.

Not many Christians are doing that. It requires effort on our part. It requires some personal sacrifice. We don't seem to have the same motivation. Yet, our motivation should be greater. We are preparing for eternity. We are facing the most serious test of all time.

As obedient children, not fashioning yourselves according to the former lusts in your ignorance: But as he which hath called you is holy, so be ye holy in all manner of conversation; Because it is written, Be ye holy; for I am holy. 1 Peter 1:14-16

We want to be fashioned like Him, in holiness. How can we do that?

And if ye call on the Father, who without respect of persons judgeth according to every man's work, pass the time of your sojourning here in fear: Forasmuch as ye know that ye were not redeemed with corruptible things, as silver and gold, from your vain conversation received by tradition from your fathers; But with the precious blood of Christ, as of a lamb without blemish and without spot: Who verily was foreordained before the foundation of the world, but was manifest in these last times for you, Who by him do believe in God, that raised him up from the dead, and gave him glory; that your faith and hope might be in God. Seeing ye have purified your souls in obeying the truth through the spirit unto unfeigned love of the brethren, see that ye love one another with a pure heart fervently:
1 Peter 1:17-22

God has called us to holiness. He is a holy God; and He desires a holy people. We can *purify our souls* by *obeying the truth* of His Word.

Being born again, not of corruptible seed, but of incorruptible, by the word of God, which liveth and abideth for ever. 1 Peter 1:23

Our original transformation in Christ was through His Word. We are *born again ... by the Word of God.* So, if the Word gives life, then the Word can sustain life, as well. Every one of us must learn this secret.

For all flesh is as grass, and all the glory of man as the flower of grass. The grass withereth, and the flower thereof falleth away: But

the word of the Lord endureth for ever. And this is the word which
by the gospel is preached unto you.   1 Peter 1:24-25

Our outer man is likened to *grass*. It only lasts for a certain period of time. Then it *withers*. Our inner man, which gets its life by the Word of God can remain forever. All of the substances which make up our bodies come from the earth. Everything we eat comes from the earth. This body is *earthy*. The spiritual man has his roots in the Word of God, *which by the gospel is preached unto you.*

As newborn babes need milk to grow, we need *the sincere milk of the Word* so that we can grow (1 Peter 2:2). Our life begins in the Word and continues in the Word. We don't need something different now. We just need another layer of the same thing, the Word of God.

Whether we hear it at church, read it at home, hear it over the radio, see it preached on television, or read it in a good book, the Word is our life.

Peter went on to speak of actually tasting the Word of God. You can *taste* the Lord. You can eat the Lord. So few Christians realize this truth in a practical sense. Theoretically, most Christians agree with this principle, but few of them take time to regularly sit down with the Word, as they do with regular physical meals, and eat.

That is why the average Christian is so weak and undernourished. We must be built up, little by little, through the Word of God. By the Word, the Christ in you is increased. By the Word, expansion takes place. You may not see it immediately; but as you continue to apply layer upon layer, the growth becomes perceptible.

Whereof I am made a minister, according to the dispensation of God
which is given to me for you, to fulfil the word of God;
                                                    Colossians 1:25

God has given us the privilege (and the responsibility) to *fulfill the Word of God.* Fulfilling the Word of God means conforming to the image of Christ. This is our goal in the Christian life. This is our privilege.

Even the mystery which hath been hid from ages and from genera-tions, but now is made manifest to his saints: To whom God would make known what is the riches of the glory of this mystery among the Gentiles; which is Christ in you, the hope of glory: Whom we preach, warning every man, and teaching every man in all wisdom; that we may present every man perfect in Christ Jesus:

Colossians 1:26-28

This word *perfect* means *mature, grown up.* The whole purpose of Paul's ministry was to bring people to spiritual maturity, to help them grow up. His goal was to *present every man perfect in Christ Jesus.*

Attending meetings will not necessarily cause you to grow. In some meetings, you may enjoy yourself. You may feel happy, as if you could jump half-way to the ceiling. At the same time, you may not be grow-ing. Growth comes through the Word of God. In many circles, the preaching of the Word of God is considered boring, and people sleep through it.

Exercising without eating properly is dangerous. Exercise is good, but it is eating that restores life. Many new Christians would like to grow instantly by the laying on of the hands of some anointed minister of God. That would be lovely, but it doesn't happen. Growth comes through the Word of God, layer upon layer.

Whereunto I also labour, striving according to his working, which worketh in me mightily. Colossians 1:29

Paul worked at it. He *laboured.* He was *striving.* This kind of growth doesn't happen without effort on our part.

In whom [Christ] are hid all the treasures of wisdom and knowl-edge. And this I say, lest any man should beguile you with enticing words. For though I be absent in the flesh, yet am I with you in the spirit, joying and beholding your order, and the stedfastness of your faith in Christ. As ye have therefore received Christ Jesus the Lord, so walk ye in him: Colossians 2:3-6

We walk in the same light that gave us birth. As we received Christ through receiving the Word, we are able to walk now by continuing to receive the Word. This is what the Christian life is all about: walking in obedience to the Word, having our hearts purified by the Word, being *rooted and built up in him* by the Word of God.

Rooted and built up in him, and stablished in the faith, as ye have been taught, abounding therein with thanksgiving.
Colossians 2:7

Abounding therein with thanksgiving. Praise is an aid to spiritual digestion. We must receive the Word with thanksgiving. When you make it a habit to praise the Lord before you eat your meals, to praise the Lord inside while you eat, and to praise the Lord after you eat, it is surprising what a tremendous aid to natural digestion it is. Exactly the same is true in the spiritual sense. We must never get tired of hearing the Word of God. It is the layer upon layer that builds us up.

Beware lest any man spoil you through philosophy and vain deceit, after the tradition of men, after the rudiments of the world, and not after Christ. For in him dwelleth all the fulness of the Godhead bodily. And ye are complete in him, which is the head of all principality and power:
Colossians 2:8-10

These are some of my favourite verses. *For in Him dwelleth all the fulness of the Godhead bodily. And ye are complete in Him.* If we are *complete* in Christ, and *in Him dwells all the fullness of the Godhead bodily,* then we have the fullness of Christ dwelling in us. Praise the Lord!

When Jesus called His disciples, formed them into apostles and sent them out, He did it through the teaching of the Word. They did not become powerful overnight. They were with Him constantly. He taught them. They asked Him questions. He cleared away their doubts. This takes time.

When they went out to minister, it was to *freely give* what they had so graciously received from Him. This took time. They taught from house to house, from village to village, from city to city, and from country to country. Slowly, layer upon layer, the Word had its effect and *Christians*, imitators of Christ, were raised up all over the known world.

The times have changed, but the process necessary to be formed into beautiful crystals that reflect the love of Jesus and that are able to withstand the most difficult times imaginable is just the same as it always was: *line upon line, precept upon precept.* Give God the time necessary for the formation of His glorious design in your life. He has destined you to become *terrible crystal.* ✸

Chapter XII

The Living Creatures Ministering As the Army of the Lord

And the likeness of the firmament upon the heads of the living creature was as the colour of the terrible crystal, stretched forth over their heads above. And under the firmament were their wings straight, the one toward the other: every one had two, which covered on this side, and every one had two, which covered on that side, their bodies. And when they went, I heard the noise of their wings, like the noise of great waters, as the voice of the almighty, the voice of speech, as the noise of an host: when they stood, they let down their wings.

Ezekiel 1:22-24

Sometimes this world is not a pretty place. It is filled with darkness and despair. Yet light shines best in darkness. Glory shines best in the midst of despair. The Church of the Lord Jesus Christ has always excelled in times of the most severe persecution and trial.

The largest Pentecostal congregation in the world today is in Seoul, Korea. Why? It has not been so very long ago that Korea was going through the most severe, distressing, appalling and terrifying of times. The hardships the Korean people faced forced millions of them to seriously seek God; and God met them in a very real way. The church in Seoul is not a witness to good times, but to what God can do for His people in hard times.

Hard times do not discourage God's people; and, if we want to be what God has called us to be, we must live the Christian life, in bad times as well as good. Historically, there have been more "bad times" for the Church than good. That has not hindered the growth and development of the Church in any sense. The Church thrives in the worst of times.

We don't like to hear it, but we can expect more bad times in the future. Prophecy declares it. This is not something that need cause us to fear. If God is with us, we have nothing to fear.

> *And they shall fall by the edge of the sword, and shall be led away captive into all nations: and Jerusalem shall be trodden down of the Gentiles, until the times of the Gentiles be fulfilled.*   Luke 21:24

When Israel became a nation in 1948, the fulfilment of *the times of the Gentiles* began. In 1967, during the Six Day War, *the times of the Gentiles* came one step closer to its end. Since then, we have been coming closer and closer to the complete fulfilment of this important prophetic period.

> *And there shall be signs in the sun, and in the moon, and in the stars; and upon the earth distress of nations, with perplexity; the sea and the waves roaring;*   Luke 21:25

Ezekiel saw the heavens filled with *terrible crystal.* Luke foresaw a time of *distress of nations with perplexity. Perplexity* speaks of seeing no way of escape. His revelation also included *signs in the sun, and in the moon, and in the stars.*

> *Men's hearts failing them for fear, and for looking after those things which are coming on the earth: for the powers of heaven shall be shaken.*   Luke 21:26

Much of this is happening already. Young people are having heart attacks, something unheard of in the past. They are concerned about the future.

> *And then shall they see the Son of man coming in a cloud with power and great glory. And when these things begin to come to pass, then look up, and lift up your heads; for your redemption draweth nigh. And he spake to them a parable; Behold the fig tree, and all the trees; When they now shoot forth, ye see and know of your own selves that summer is now nigh at hand. So likewise ye, when ye see these things come to pass, know ye that the kingdom of God is nigh at hand. Verily I say unto you, This generation shall not pass away, till all be fulfilled. Heaven and earth shall pass away: but my words shall not pass away. And take heed to yourselves, lest at any time your hearts be overcharged with surfeiting, and drunkenness, and cares of this life, and so that day come upon you unawares. For as a snare shall it come on all them that dwell on the face of the whole earth. Watch ye therefore, and pray always, that ye may be ac-counted worthy to escape all these things that shall come to pass, and to stand before the Son of man.* Luke 21:27-36

This passage needs no explanation. Those who know anything at all about the world in which we are living know that these things are already happening. This is truly a day of *surfeiting and drunkenness*. The vast majority of people in our Western society are overtaken with *the cares of this life*.

This is the day of which Jesus warned us. He said: *Take heed to your-selves. Take heed!* The events which Jesus describes will come *as a snare*, an unexpected trap, upon people all over the world. *Take heed!* Don't be caught in the trap. Be prepared. Get ready.

Who knows how long we will have the freedoms we are now enjoy-ing. Historically, times of such peace have been relatively few. This period may pass at any moment, and without warning.

My own daughter-in-law and her mother and sister woke up one morning in Shanghai, China, looked out the window and saw Com-munist soldiers standing at intervals of a few feet outside their home. They had entered the city and taken up their positions overnight.

These things happen. For some years now we have been talking about them happening in other places. But who knows when they will happen outside our homes too. *Take heed!*

> *Yea, and all that will live godly in Christ Jesus shall suffer persecution. But evil men and seducers shall wax worse and worse, deceiving, and being deceived. But continue thou in the things which thou hast learned and hast been assured of, knowing of whom thou hast learned them; And that from a child thou hast known the holy scriptures, which are able to make thee wise unto salvation through faith which is in Christ Jesus.*   2 Timothy 3:12-15

The world is not getting better and better, as some believe. It is getting worse and worse. This should not surprise us. These things have happened many times in the past and will happen again in the near future. The Scriptures are able to make us wise enough to avoid the consequences of such an occurrence.

> *All scripture is given by inspiration of God, and is profitable for doctrine, for reproof, for correction, for instruction in righteousness: That the man of God may be perfect, throughly furnished unto all good works.*   2 Timothy 3:16-17

We can be perfected by receiving the teachings of the Scriptures. We can be *furnished unto all good works* by receiving the teachings of the Scriptures. We can be prepared for anything that may happen in the future by receiving the teachings of the Scriptures.

> *I charge thee therefore before God, and the Lord Jesus Christ, who shall judge the quick and the dead at his appearing and his kingdom; Preach the word; be instant in season, out of season; reprove, rebuke, exhort with all longsuffering and doctrine.*   2 Timothy 4:1-2

We are not commanded to preach "about the Word", as many are doing. We are commanded to *preach the Word*. One day, when I stand before God, I will be so glad that I have been faithful in this regard. I have never stopped preaching the Word of God.

For the time will come when they will not endure sound doctrine; but after their own lusts shall they heap to themselves teachers, having itching ears; And they shall turn away their ears from the truth, and shall be turned unto fables. But watch thou in all things, endure afflictions, do the work of an evangelist, make full proof of thy ministry. For I am now ready to be offered, and the time of my departure is at hand. I have fought a good fight, I have finished my course, I have kept the faith: Henceforth there is laid up for me a crown of righteousness, which the Lord, the righteous judge, shall give me at that day: and not to me only, but unto all them also that love his appearing.   2 Timothy 4:3-8

When I visited Rome, I went to see the great Colosseum. As I stood there, beholding that ancient ruin and listening to the stories of the Christians who were kept there in small cells, waiting their turn to face the lions, tears streamed down my cheeks. There is still a very holy presence of the Lord in that place where so many believers joyfully met their death.

Paul was not trying to frighten Timothy. He was being very realistic. He knew that he himself would have to face such things and that Timothy, also, needed to be prepared for whatever life brought his way. Paul could not always be by Timothy's side, and one day he would make his *departure.* He rested in the fact that he had *fought a good fight, finished* [the] *course,* and *kept the faith.*

The man who was used of God to establish the Gentile churches and write over half of the New Testament was *ready to be offered.* He didn't have to wait long. His death, however, did not mean the end of the Church. It was in her darkest hour that the Church shone brightest and had her greatest success in winning souls. Are we ready for a repeat of first-century history?

Ezekiel saw our day as awesome. The prophet Joel foresaw our day, as well, and described what God showed him:

The word of the Lord that came to Joel the son of Pethuel. Hear this, ye old men, and give ear, all ye inhabitants of the land. Hath this been in your days, or even in the days of your fathers? Tell ye your children of it, and let your children tell their children, and their children another generation. That which the palmerworm hath left hath the locust eaten; and that which the locust hath left hath the cankerworm eaten; and that which the cankerworm hath left hath the caterpiller eaten. Awake, ye drunkards, and weep; and howl, all ye drinkers of wine, because of the new wine; for it is cut off from your mouth. For a nation is come up upon my land, strong, and without number, whose teeth are the teeth of a lion, and he hath the cheek teeth of a great lion. He hath laid my vine waste, and barked my fig tree: he hath made it clean bare, and cast it away; the branches thereof are made white. Lament like a virgin girded with sackcloth for the husband of her youth. The meat offering and the drink offering is cut off from the house of the Lord; the priests, the Lord's ministers, mourn. The field is wasted, the land mourneth; for the corn is wasted: the new wine is dried up, the oil languisheth. Be ye ashamed, O ye husbandmen; howl, O ye vinedressers, for the wheat and for the barley; because the harvest of the field is perished. The vine is dried up, and the fig tree languisheth; the pomegranate tree, the palm tree also, and the apple tree, even all the trees of the field, are withered: because joy is withered away from the sons of men.

Joel 1:1-12

This is the appalling and shocking day of which Joel prophesied. We are starving to death in a country full of Bibles. Churches have ceased to offer a pleasing sacrifice to the Lord. Worship has become distorted and abused. The anointing of the Holy Ghost *(the oil)* is in very short supply.

This is a time of shame, a time to *mourn and howl. Joy is withered away from the sons of men.* This is serious. Our joy is our strength. We cannot afford to allow our joy to wither. Joel calls for action.

Gird yourselves, and lament, ye priests: howl, ye ministers of the altar: come, lie all night in sackcloth, ye ministers of my God: for the meat offering and the drink offering is withholden from the house of your God. Sanctify ye a fast, call a solemn assembly, gather the

*elders and all the inhabitants of the land into the house of the Lord
your God, and cry unto the Lord,* Joel 1:13-14

All is not lost. Our God can turn things around for His people. But
we must stir ourselves to seek Him. We must reclaim the joy and the
anointing *(the oil* and *the new wine).* We must return to a healthy diet of
corn and meat in order to be strong soldiers for the Lord's battle.

The Church is not destined for defeat. It is destined for victory. The
Church does not depend on prevailing world conditions for her peace.
Jesus Christ is her peace, whatever the prevailing world conditions
might be.

The *palmerworm* which Joel mentioned is a caterpillar which gets its
name from its wandering habits. *Palmer* means *pilgrim.* The English
word originated with the return of pilgrims from the Holy Land bearing palms as a souvenir. Later, the Scottish people used the word to
mean *to wander about or to be a vagrant.*

Joel foresaw that vagrants, those who just wander from church to
church without commitment, would do much damage to the existing
church. Wanderers are not used by God. They are not stable.

What would you think of a person who decided to sleep in a different house each night or a person who decided to work for a different
company every week? Would you have any confidence in their judgment? Would you ask for their help in making important decisions?

I think we need to get serious in the House of God. Perhaps we need
to install a time clock and have people punch their card when they
come and go. If you don't do it at work, you don't get paid.

That which the palmerworm hath left hath the locust eaten: Those of you
who are old enough to remember the "Dirty Thirties" know the desperation people faced when the little that was left of the harvest,
because of the terrible drought, was eaten by swarms of locusts. I was
fortunate enough to be living in a part of Manitoba where we didn't
suffer from either curse.

Those were terrible days; and there were no welfare agencies for
those living in the countryside. They had to band together and help
one another. If anyone had a few extra vegetables, they would take

them to the railroad station, and the Canadian Pacific Railroad would deliver them free of charge to those who were in need.

People didn't have much in those days, but they had big hearts. Now, some are dumping vegetables in the river to keep the price artificially high. More food is thrown in the garbage now than people had to eat during those difficult times.

Swarms of demons have emerged upon the earth and are destroying the spiritual growth of the Church. There are spirits of delusion and discouragement.

That which the locust hath left hath the cankerworm eaten: The cankerworm attacks trees and destroys their leaves so that there is no fruit. The *canker sore* comes from the same word. It is an ulcer-like sore that spreads. Do not let a *cankerworm* eat at you. If the devil cannot destroy God's people any other way, he will get at them through something that eats at their insides. It gnaws away, spreading as it goes.

You may wake up one day feeling fine, but then you begin to wonder why 'so and so' did 'such and such'. Someone says something to you because 'so and so' thinks that 'so and so' said something they shouldn't have. And before you know it, the *cankerworm* is eating away at you. If you are like most people, you have experienced that very thing. The whole episode left you edgy, upset and disturbed.

That which the cankerworm hath left hath the caterpiller eaten: Caterpillars can be very destructive. May God help us. These are the forces at work in the Church today.

It is time for drunkards to *awake,* to *weep and howl.* We cannot have God's new wine in our lives if we are in a stupor with the world's brew.

The *lion* of which Joel spoke is stalking the land. He is *strong.* His *teeth* are vicious. He will devour all who are in a weakened condition and cannot escape him. The vines have been *laid waste.* The fig trees have been *barked* so that they cannot grow normally and produce.

This is serious, and we need to recognize just how serious it is. God tells us to *lament like a virgin girded with sackcloth for the husband of her youth.* Things are not getting better, they are getting worse. Wake up, Church! The day of which Joel prophesied is here.

What should we do?

Blow ye the trumpet in Zion, and sound an alarm in my holy mountain: let all the inhabitants of the land tremble: for the day of the Lord cometh, for it is nigh at hand; A day of darkness and of gloominess, a day of clouds and of thick darkness, as the morning spread upon the mountains: a great people and a strong; there hath not been ever the like, neither shall be any more after it, even to the years of many generations. A fire devoureth before them; and behind them a flame burneth: the land is as the garden of Eden before them, and behind them a desolate wilderness; yea, and nothing shall escape them. The appearance of them is as the appearance of horses; and as horsemen, so shall they run. Like the noise of chariots on the tops of mountains shall they leap, like the noise of a flame of fire that devoureth the stubble, as a strong people set in battle array. Before their face the people shall be much pained: all faces shall gather blackness. They shall run like mighty men; they shall climb the wall like men of war; and they shall march every one on his ways, and they shall not break their ranks: Neither shall one thrust another; they shall walk every one in his path: and when they fall upon the sword, they shall not be wounded. They shall run to and fro in the city; they shall run upon the wall, they shall climb up upon the houses; they shall enter in at the windows like a thief. The earth shall quake before them; the heavens shall tremble: the sun and the moon shall be dark, and the stars shall withdraw their shining: And the Lord shall utter his voice before his army: for his camp is very great: for he is strong that executeth his word: for the day of the Lord is great and very terrible; and who can abide it? Joel 2:1-11

Joel saw some of the same things that Ezekiel saw, a time of darkness, gloominess, cloudiness, and thick darkness. But in the midst of that darkness, God revealed a great and strong people. That's us. Like it or not, God has destined us to shine in gross darkness, to be His *terrible crystal* in the face of fearsome events which are about to unfold upon the earth. Get ready for it, Army of the Lord.

One of the most important things Joel said about this strong army was that *they shall not break their ranks*. There will be no division in this army. These strong men are *as one*. No wonder the earth will *quake* before this army! No wonder the heavens will *tremble!* When we become united, nothing can stop us.

How do we get ready for such a day?

> *Therefore also now, saith the Lord, turn ye even to me with all your heart, and with fasting, and with weeping, and with mourning: And rend your heart, and not your garments, and turn unto the Lord your God: for he is gracious and merciful, slow to anger, and of great kindness, and repenteth him of the evil. Who knoweth if he will return and repent, and leave a blessing behind him; even a meat offering and a drink offering unto the Lord your God? Blow the trumpet in Zion, sanctify a fast, call a solemn assembly: Gather the people, sanctify the congregation, assemble the elders, gather the children, and those that suck the breasts: let the bridegroom go forth of his chamber, and the bride out of her closet.*   Joel 2:12-16

This is a family affair. There are babies in this army and small children. The elderly have their place in this army, as well. This great army is made up of all of God's children.

We cannot afford to abandon our youth today. They may have many struggles in life, but God has reserved a place for them in His army. Young people have an important role to play in God's plans for the future. Even the very smallest children are not excluded. Be patient with the young ones. Nurture them, don't criticize them. They will grow — if we give them a chance and feed them properly.

When the people of Israel marched out of Egypt, they came out by families. Whole families had to march together through the wilderness, the very young and the very old included. But God gave them strength. Not one grandfather or one grandmother was left beside the road. No children were abandoned because they couldn't keep up with the march. Those whom we would think of as weak were certainly not airlifted to the front. Everyone had to walk. Yet the Scriptures declare:

> *He brought them forth also with silver and gold: and there was not one feeble person among their tribes.*   Psalms 105:37

What a miracle! *There was not one feeble person among their tribes.* God can do that for us again today. He wants to use everyone in this end-time army.

We should be faithful to those things God has called us to do in regard to fasting as an assembly, and we should also be faithful to those things that God has called us to do personally with regard to fasting. We must assemble ourselves for prayer, and we need regular and consistent fasting.

Some people are abandoning the practice of fasting altogether. This is tragic. Never take a step backward in your Christian life. Let us be faithful to the call of God.

> *Let the priests, the ministers of the Lord, weep between the porch and the altar, and let them say, Spare thy people, O Lord, and give not thine heritage to reproach, that the heathen should rule over them: wherefore should they say among the people, Where is their God?* Joel 2:17

This should be our cry today! This should be our prayer for the saints of God! *Spare Thy People, O Lord, and give not thine heritage to reproach.* When people backslide, they become a reproach to the name of Jesus Christ. When a person who professes to be saved continues to live in sin, he or she is a reproach to the name of Jesus Christ. When a child of God refuses to give up fleshly and carnal habits, he or she is a reproach to the name of Jesus Christ. We must pray that our spiritual heritage not be given to reproach. The heathen have no right to rule over us.

Let us pray that faith be increased. A little bit goes a long way. Faith as a grain of mustard seed still moves mountains. God did a miracle by faith in 1952, by shortening my right leg two inches; and He is still doing miracles forty-one years later. Don't lose your faith. Although the world has changed, God has not.

> *Then will the Lord be jealous for his land, and pity his people. Yea, the Lord will answer and say unto his people, Behold, I will send you corn, and wine, and oil, and ye shall be satisfied therewith: and I will no more make you a reproach among the heathen:* Joel 2:18-19

God is ready to move on behalf of His children. He is ready to remove the reproach of the past. He is ready to restore *the corn, the wine and the oil.* He is only waiting for us to *blow the trumpet, sanctify a fast and call a solemn assembly.* He is waiting for us to react to the terrible times in which we live. *Then will the Lord be jealous for His land, and pity His people.* When will He do this? When we start obeying Him.

He is ready and waiting to do it. He will send us *corn,* the good richness of His Word. He will send us *wine,* the joy of the Holy Ghost. He will send us *oil,* the anointing of the Holy Ghost. He will remove our reproach among the heathen.

The forces of the Enemy want to strip you of your leaves, like the destructive worms that Joel saw in his vision. They want to leave you bare and defenceless. They want to spoil the growth of the children of God. Trees can't grow properly if they constantly have their leaves stripped from them. And you can't grow if the Enemy is constantly stripping away your life.

Some ministers seem to specialize in stripping people. I don't believe, however, that this is the ministry of Jesus Christ. It's okay to help people say good-bye to wrong and to evil, but it cannot be correct to make them feel like they have nothing left.

The ministry that interests God is to clothe His people, to put fat on their bones. He will do it if we seek Him. *Seek the Lord, and ye shall live.* The Enemy is strengthening himself for battle. We must do the same. We don't want him to take everything that we have. He fully intends to take our furniture, to take our food, to take our houses, and to take our money.

Satan is the master Spoiler. He enters where he doesn't belong and takes anything we will allow him to take. Don't allow him to send you a spirit of drowsiness. That's one of his tricks. He gets you drowsy, and then he can steal whatever he wants. Don't sit back while he devastates your health and the health and well-being of your family. Rise up and go after the Intruder. Take back what is rightfully yours.

And the likeness of the firmament upon the heads of the living creature was as the colour of the terrible crystal, stretched forth over their heads above.   Ezekiel 1:22

Those who trust the Lord will see a very different type of day than those who have refused Him. For those who love the Lord and are walking in His ways, there is nothing to fear. Our God reigns — whatever else happens.

> *The Lord reigneth; let the earth rejoice; let the multitude of isles be glad thereof. Clouds and darkness are round about him: righteousness and judgment are the habitation of his throne. A fire goeth before him, and burneth up his enemies round about. His lightnings enlightened the world: the earth saw, and trembled. The hills melted like wax at the presence of the Lord, at the presence of the Lord of the whole earth. The heavens declare his righteousness, and all the people see his glory.* Psalms 97:1-6

Clouds and darkness are round about Him, but He still reigns. When confusion and chaos are the order of the day, our God is still in charge. He still holds the whole world in His hand. He reigns — in the face of every circumstance.

David continued.

> *For thou, Lord, art high above all the earth: thou art exalted far above all gods. Ye that love the Lord, hate evil: he preserveth the souls of his saints; he delivereth them out of the hand of the wicked.* Psalms 97:9-10

This is the same vision that Joel saw and Ezekiel saw. The Psalmist saw that God's people would not be affected by that which destroyed others at their side. *He preserveth the souls of His saints,* he assured. *He delivereth them out of the hand of the wicked.*

> *Light is sown for the righteous, and gladness for the upright in heart. Rejoice in the Lord, ye righteous; and give thanks at the remembrance of his holiness.* Psalms 97:11-12

It is the same picture over and over again. The time of God's reign over His people will be glorious. His glory will shine in the midst of darkness. His light will prevail in the midst of gloom.

Ezekiel saw the same picture. He saw the living creatures, the Body of Jesus Christ, and heard the noise of their wings *like the noise of great waters* (Ezekiel 1:24). This speaks of their movement, their activity, their ministry. We don't have to be devastated by the terrible things that are coming on the earth. We can be victorious and go on to minister victory to others.

The vision of Joel ended on a victorious note. He saw a church besieged. He called that church to fasting and prayer and seeking God in seriousness. But then he saw a good result in the end.

He said, *"And it shall come to pass afterward ..."* (Joel 2:28). When we recognize the seriousness of our condition and start doing something about it, God honours that and moves on our behalf, by the Spirit. Ezekiel saw the living creatures with great activity, with a noisy "busyness". Joel saw us preparing for war.

> *Proclaim ye this among the Gentiles; prepare war, wake up the mighty men, let all the men of war draw near; let them come up: Beat your plowshares into swords and your pruninghooks into spears: let the weak say, I am strong.* Joel 3:9-10

It is time for the weak to say, *I am strong*. Humility does not demand that we accept our nothingness. In true humility, we can be somebody, but we know that what we are depends totally on the Lord. In these last days, we must cast off weakness and accept the strength of the Lord.

"How can we be strong when we're so weak?" you might ask.

I would answer: "We will be strong because He is strong. His strength will become our strength. We can say that we are strong because He is living in us, and He is strong."

> *Put ye in the sickle, for the harvest is ripe: come, get you down; for the press is full, the fats overflow; for their wickedness is great. Multitudes, multitudes in the valley of decision: for the day of the Lord is near in the valley of decision. The sun and the moon shall be darkened, and the stars shall withdraw their shining. The Lord also shall roar out of Zion, and utter his voice from Jerusalem; and the*

heavens and the earth shall shake: but the Lord will be the hope of his people, and the strength of the children of Israel. So shall ye know that I am the Lord your God dwelling in Zion, my holy mountain: then shall Jerusalem be holy, and there shall no strangers pass through her any more.   Joel 3:13-17

The Lord is about to *roar out of Zion.* Get ready for it. Let Him be your hope. Let Him be your strength. He is *dwelling in Zion.* Zion is the house of the Lord, His people. He lives in us. And He is not just our guest. He owns the house. He is the Creator of all things. He is Master of all. Let Him have His way.

Let the Lion of the Tribe of Judah roar! If His roar frightens some, it will do them good.

In the Garden of Eden, God gave Adam and Eve dominion over all the earth. Everything was to be subdued under them. Through their rebellion, they lost that dominion; but this is the restoration for which Jesus Christ paid. We can know the power that Adam and Eve experienced. We can receive the knowledge of God, as Adam and Eve received it. We can have dominion, just as Adam and Eve had.

Adam was a glorious creation. His ability to intelligently name all the animals is just an indication of his vast mental capacity. God wants to restore to us what Adam lost.

Adam's sin forced him from the protecting arms of God and under the power of the Evil One. God wants to be our protection — in the midst of the most difficult circumstances imaginable.

He that dwelleth in the secret place of the most High shall abide under the shadow of the Almighty. I will say of the Lord, He is my refuge and my fortress: my God; in him will I trust. Surely he shall deliver thee from the snare of the fowler, and from the noisome pestilence. He shall cover thee with his feathers, and under his wings shalt thou trust: his truth shall be thy shield and buckler.
                                                    Psalms 91:1-4

The living creatures were *covered* with their wings. The anointing of the Lord was upon them, and they had nothing to fear.

Most everyone has heard the now-famous story of the soldier in World War II who was shot, but who was not harmed. His Bible in his pocket protected him. The bullet stopped at Psalms 91.

Thou shalt not be afraid for the terror by night; nor for the arrow that flieth by day;   Psalms 91:5

The devil has launched a campaign of fear. He is the author of fear. Fear is not of God. If Satan can succeed in causing us to fear, he can prevent us from working and from ministering as God would have us to do. Fear is a paralysing force. Fight fear with faith. Faith is the victory. *Have faith in God.*

Nor for the pestilence that walketh in darkness; nor for the destruction that wasteth at noonday. A thousand shall fall at thy side, and ten thousand at thy right hand; but it shall not come nigh thee. Only with thine eyes shalt thou behold and see the reward of the wicked. Because thou hast made the Lord, which is my refuge, even the most High, thy habitation; There shall no evil befall thee, neither shall any plague come nigh thy dwelling.   Psalms 91:6-10

That soldier I mentioned was in the middle of a fierce battle, but he himself was not wounded. God's power to protect us in the midst of danger is very real. This passage is so marvellous that every believer should memorize it. If you can get things straight in your mind, the heart will follow. God has even promised that no *plague* will come near our *dwelling*. Because we have made God our *habitation*, nothing will harm us.

If ye then be risen with Christ, seek those things which are above, where Christ sitteth on the right hand of God.   Colossians 3:1

See yourself as God sees you. You are a spiritual creation. You are *seated in the heavenlies.* You have wings that protect you from any danger. You have nothing to fear.

A young brother who had been backslidden told me what happened during a power failure. He and another young man were in a beer parlour. When the lights went out, the young fellow thought the Lord had come and went running around with a glass of beer in his hand screaming, "The Lord has come! The Lord has come!" The problem was he was still hanging onto the glass of beer. That is not the reaction the Lord is looking for in us. He wants us to *seek those things which are above.* Many people are determined to let go of their sins — when the Lord comes. As we see by this example, it will be too late then. Now is the time to draw near to God and to come under His protection.

For ye are dead, and your life is hid with Christ in God.
Colossians 3:3

You are *in Christ,* and Christ is *in God.* You have nothing to fear. Anything that comes against you must first come against the armour of God. If it got past God, it would have to face the armour of Christ before it could get to you. You are safe. No evil can befall you. That is God's promise.

Once, a couple was having a problem with a neighbour poisoning their kittens. They were both Christians and were determined to call the heavenly police. I prayed by faith and put a blood line around their property, without even going there. From that day on, their neighbour could not come near them. They never had another problem.

This is the promise of God. *No evil shall befall thee.* Plagues won't be able to come near your *dwelling.* This is insurance against evil and against sickness. This is insurance against flu bugs. This is better than a vaccination.

For he shall give his angels charge over thee, to keep thee in all thy ways. They shall bear thee up in their hands, lest thou dash thy foot against a stone. Thou shalt tread upon the lion and adder: the young lion and the dragon shalt thou trample under feet. Because he hath set his love upon me, therefore will I deliver him: I will set him on high, because he hath known my name. He shall call upon me, and I will answer him: I will be with him in trouble; I will deliver him, and honour him. With long life will I satisfy him, and shew him my salvation. Psalms 91:11-16

He hath known my name. Some people are so willing and ready to blame God for someone being in an accident or someone dying. But God is not in the killing business. He gives life. *With long life I will satisfy him.* Believe it. Don't expect to die before your time. Don't expect to contract some rare disease. Don't expect to have an accident. Expect God to save you from every enemy. He has promised to do it.

When we know that God is protecting us, we can praise Him. We must do it, for praise works. He does *inhabit the praises* of His people. Praise demonstrates faith in His promises. When I feel a special need in my household, I just go around the house praising God, and demons have to flee in every direction.

If the devil can put fear in your life, you will stop praising God. You cannot allow that to happen. If fear tries to creep into you, make a desperate effort to praise God anyway. It works better than rebuking the devil. He gets nervous when you start praising God. Let him hear your praises:

"Thank You, Jesus."
"Praise You, Jesus, for the Blood."
"Glory! Hallelujah!"

Let me tell you: when the spirit of fear hears those words, he will run every time. These are good things to know!

When Ezekiel saw the living creatures, their wings were not shaking with fear. They were *straight.*

We are living in the day when the army of God must go forth and reclaim all that the Enemy has stolen. We have nothing to fear. God is on our side. As the signs in heaven become more fearful and the events on earth more shocking, we must remember that the Christ-likeness of the Christian is also expanding. We are becoming the likeness of the living creatures on earth. And we are bearing the image of the heavenly.

The likeness of the heaven above our heads is causing great fear *(terrible crystal),* and it is expanding, more distressing, not less frightening. However, the likeness of the living creatures is relating with the expansion above their heads.

The first man is of the earth, earthy: the second man is the Lord from heaven. As is the earthy, such are they also that are earthy: and as is the heavenly, such are they also that are heavenly. And as we have borne the image of the earthy, we shall also bear the image of the heavenly. I Corinthians 15:47-49

We have become *terrible crystal*.

Chapter XIII

Resting in God

And there was a voice from the firmament that was over their heads,
when they stood, and had let down their wings.   Ezekiel 1:25

In this verse we see the living creatures resting. They *had let down their wings*. God knows that His mighty army, which moves about and is very active for His cause, needs time to rest. There is a time, therefore, to march forward; and there is a time to rest.

Those who are not properly rested will have difficulty keeping step with this army. It is not wise to be worn out before the battle even begins. We must learn to rest in God.

A bird, when it has let down its wings, is immobile. It ceases activity for a while — to eat or to rest. We must learn to do the same. Going forward is important, but resting is just as important.

Some people can pray around the clock but still not accomplish as much for God as those who pray half-way around the clock. They are very busy, but busy in their own strength. I have learned to refuse to ask God over and over again for the things I need. I refuse to insult Him in that way. He knows what I need. I let down my wings and wait for His answer.

Let us therefore fear, lest, a promise being left us of entering into his rest, any of you should seem to come short of it. For unto us was the gospel preached, as well as unto them: but the word preached did not profit them, not being mixed with faith in them that heard it. For we which have believed do enter into rest, as he said, As I have sworn in my wrath, if they shall enter into my rest: although the works were finished from the foundation of the world. For he spake in a certain place of the seventh day on this wise, And God did rest the seventh day from all his works. Hebrews 4:1-4

We have the *promise ... of entering into His rest.* This rest seems to have something to do with our faith. Rest is rejuvenating. It rids us of the toxins in our system (the tensions, doubts and fears). It prepares us to receive. It provides the digestive juices for spiritual eating.

Because many have learned the biblical truth that faith without works is dead, they think they have to be feverishly producing something every minute of every day. They become overworked because they are not renewing themselves through the Holy Ghost. Resting in God doesn't mean you don't have faith. Just the opposite is true. Having faith allows you to rest in God.

There remaineth therefore a rest to the people of God. Hebrews 4:9

If the devil had his way, he would run you ragged and destroy your nerves. God wants to give you rest, to restore you for battle. Know Him and believe Him, and you can rest in Him.

For he that is entered into his rest, he also hath ceased from his own works, as God did from his. Hebrews 4:10

I remember the time my dear husband hid his wallet one Sunday morning (after having too much to drink the night before). I would not have cared except for the fact that all that was remaining of his week's pay was in there. I wanted some money, so I awakened him and asked him for his wallet. (At that time of his life, he usually slept all day Sunday until I awakened him for dinner at five o'clock.)

"I hid it," he said, "You'll never find it."

"The Lord will find it for me," I replied. But as soon as I had said those words, I realized that I was now forced to find the wallet. I spent all the time between morning service and 2:30 Sunday school looking for it, but I could not find it.

After Sunday school, I went into the prayer room and prayed desperately that God would have mercy on me and show me where the wallet was. I had used every available moment at home, searching for that wallet. I dreaded waking my husband for the evening meal, only to have him say: "I told you so." I felt as if I would be failing God. I had, after all, said that He would show me where it was.

When I got home, I searched one more time, then I gave up (I ceased from my own works). I said: "Lord, I simply cannot find it. I give up." When I did that, I received, in an instant, what I now know to be a word of knowledge in a vision. I instantly knew where the wallet was. He had hidden it well, in a bathroom that we shared with the couple in the adjoining suite. Who would have thought that he would put it in a public place? But God knew.

I went into the bathroom and put my hand into a small space that God had shown me behind the bathtub, and there it was. I took all the money out of the wallet and laid it on the dresser empty. After my husband woke up and saw it, he never said another word.

When I ceased from my own works, God took action. We must learn to stand on God's Word, let down our wings, and rest in the Holy Ghost.

Let us labour therefore to enter into that rest, lest any man fall after the same example of unbelief. For the word of God is quick, and powerful, and sharper than any twoedged sword, piercing even to the dividing asunder of soul and spirit, and of the joints and marrow, and is a discerner of the thoughts and intents of the heart.
Hebrews 4:11-12

Let us labour therefore to enter into that rest. This seems like a contradiction: labour in order to rest. But it is just that way. There is a conscious effort on our part needed in the exercise of our faith. When you believe, you rest. You know that *the word of God is quick, and powerful.* Because the Word of God is operative and effective, we are able to rest in it.

Let us compare Joshua and Elijah in this respect. Joshua was the man God chose to lead His people into the promised land and to possess it.

> *Moses my servant is dead; now therefore arise, go over this Jordan, thou, and all this people, unto the land which I do give to them, even to the children of Israel.* Joshua 1:2

God commanded Joshua to do an impossible thing: *arise, go over this Jordan.* The thing was impossible to Joshua, but not to God. Therefore, Joshua could not do it in his own strength.

> *Every place that the sole of your foot shall tread upon, that have I given unto you, as I said unto Moses.* Joshua 1:3

They were not to take just any land. God carefully defined the borders of the land they were to possess. Then, He said:

> *There shall not any man be able to stand before thee all the days of thy life: as I was with Moses, so I will be with thee: I will not fail thee, nor forsake thee. Be strong and of a good courage: for unto this people shalt thou divide for an inheritance the land, which I sware unto their fathers to give them. Only be thou strong and very courageous, that thou mayest observe to do according to all the law, which Moses my servant commanded thee: turn not from it to the right hand or to the left, that thou mayest prosper whithersoever thou goest. This book of the law shall not depart out of thy mouth; but thou shalt meditate therein day and night, that thou mayest observe to do according to all that is written therein: for then thou shalt make thy way prosperous, and then thou shalt have good success. Have not I commanded thee? Be strong and of a good*

*courage; be not afraid, neither be thou dismayed: for the Lord thy
God is with thee whithersoever thou goest.*   Joshua 1:5-9

My daughter, Julie, was the valedictorian of her senior class in high
school. For her address, she chose Joshua 1:8. That message spoke
forcefully to the Chief of Police, Chris Enfield, and to others who were
present in the high school auditorium that night. They came to me and
said, "My, you must be proud of your daughter." I was, and I was
proud of my God who takes the words of our mouths and makes them
reality, confirming His Word by what He does in and through us.

God surely gave Julie *good success.* He paid every penny of her five
years of university education.

God exhorted Joshua not to let *this word* depart from his mouth. He
was to *meditate therein day and night.* He was to eat the Word, then he
was to act upon the Word: *that thou mayest observe to do according to all
that is written therein.* This is the secret of success. God has promised it.

Joshua prepared to go forth in obedience to the command of God.
The Ark, symbol of the presence of the Lord, was to go before
the people.

*And Joshua said unto the people, Sanctify yourselves: for to morrow
the Lord will do wonders among you. And Joshua spake unto the
priests, saying, Take up the ark of the covenant, And pass over
before the people. And they took up the ark of the covenant, and went
before the people. And the Lord said unto Joshua, This day will I
begin to magnify thee in the sight of all Israel, that they may know
that, as I was with Moses, so I will be with thee. And thou shalt
command the priests that bear the ark of the covenant, saying, When
ye are come to the brink of the water of Jordan, ye shall stand still in
Jordan.*

Joshua 3:5-8

The priests that bore His presence were to *stand still* in the midst of
the river that was to receive the miracle working power of God, to
stand still in the midst of the river that was to be used by God to make
a way into the promised land.

God told King Jehoshaphat through His prophet, *Stand ye still, and see the salvation of the Lord.*

> *Behold, the ark of the covenant of the Lord of all the earth passeth over before you into Jordan. Now therefore take you twelve men out of the tribes of Israel, out of every tribe a man. And it shall come to pass, as soon as the soles of the feet of the priests that bear the ark of the Lord, the Lord of all the earth, shall rest in the waters of Jordan, that the waters of Jordan shall be cut off from the waters that come down from above; and they shall stand upon an heap*
> Joshua 3:11-13

God's way into the promised land was made by the walking of the priesthood anointed with His presence upon their shoulders. Hallelujah! They were to walk into His promised miracle and stay there (the sole of their feet resting in the River Jordan).

> *And as they that bare the ark were come unto Jordan, and the feet of the priests that bare the ark were dipped in the brim of the water, (for Jordan overfloweth all his banks all the time of harvest,) That the waters which came down from above stood and rose up upon an heap very far from the city Adam, that is beside Zaretan: and those that came down toward the sea of the plain, even the salt sea, failed, and were cut off: and the people passed over right against Jericho. And the priests that bare the ark of the covenant of the Lord stood firm on dry ground in the midst of Jordan, and all the Israelites passed over on dry ground, until all the people were passed clean over Jordan.*
> Joshua 3:15-17

The waters of the Jordan backed up all the way to the First Adam, the head of the human race, making a way where there was no way, as the Last Adam, Jesus Christ, stood in the waters to do the impossible for His people.

Ezekiel, God's priest in captivity, was learning as he saw the vision.

*And there was a voice from the firmament that was over their heads,
when they stood, and had let down their wings.* Ezekiel 1:25

Lord, help us to do the same.

*And it came to pass, when Joshua was by Jericho, that he lifted up
his eyes and looked, and, behold, there stood a man over against him
with his sword drawn in his hand: and Joshua went unto him, and
said unto him, Art thou for us, or for our adversaries? And he said,
Nay; but as captain of the host of the Lord am I now come. And
Joshua fell on his face to the earth, and did worship, and said unto
him, What saith my lord unto his servant? And the captain of the
Lord's host said unto Joshua, Loose thy shoe from off thy foot; for the
place whereon thou standest is holy. And Joshua did so.*
Joshua 5:13-15

Are you for us or our adversaries? Jesus Christ, *the same yesterday, today
and forever,* straightened His shoulders, lifted His head, looked at His
lieutenant, Joshua, and said, "I am Captain of the Lord's host, and I am
come to give you instructions as to how to defeat Jericho.

How was Joshua to defeat a walled city? How was he to win the
battle when he had no trained military people and no precise weapons? No mention was made of armour or the number of men to deploy
on each flank or which type of arrows to use.

*Now Jericho was straitly shut up because of the children of Israel:
none went out, and none came in. And the Lord said unto Joshua,
See, I have given into thine hand Jericho, and the king thereof, and
the mighty men of valour. And ye shall compass the city, all ye men
of war, and go round about the city once. Thus shalt thou do six
days. And seven priests shall bear before the ark seven trumpets of
rams' horns: and the seventh day ye shall compass the city seven
times, and the priests shall blow with the trumpets. And it shall
come to pass, that when they make a long blast with the ram's horn,
and when ye hear the sound of the trumpet, all the people shall shout*

with a great shout; and the wall of the city shall fall down flat, and
the people shall ascend up every man straight before him.
Joshua 6:1-5

These were the orders given by the Captain of the Lord's host — no talking! Just walking, walking in faith that not one enemy could harm them, and resting in the power of the orders of their Captain. They had a "march past" before the Lord, and this carried them through for each day.

And it came to pass, when Joshua had spoken unto the people, that
the seven priests bearing the seven trumpets of rams' horns passed
on before the Lord, and blew with the trumpets: and the ark of the
covenant of the Lord followed them.   Joshua 6:8

In April of 1967, I was in Cairo, Egypt. (The Six-Day War broke out in June.) The guns that were visible everywhere made us feel very uneasy. It is not pleasant to have weapons aimed at you.

When we got to Jerusalem, I wanted a picture of the gate that divided the city (not realizing that it would soon disappear). I had my son's movie camera. When I raised my camera slightly above the gate, I looked right into the muzzle of some guns pointed my way. It didn't take me long to put the camera away.

Joshua needed real courage to rest under these circumstances. But he did, marching around each day without a word. Then, on the seventh day, they marched around seven times, and the walls fell down, just as the Lord had said they would.

Once again Joshua could hear the word that the Lord had spoken to him:

Every place that the sole of your foot shall tread upon, that have I
given unto you, as I said unto Moses.
There shall not any man be able to stand before thee all the days of
thy life: as I was with Moses, so I will be with thee: I will not fail thee,
nor forsake thee.

This book of the law shall not depart out of thy mouth; but thou shalt meditate therein day and night, that thou mayest observe to do according to all that is written therein: for then thou shalt make thy way prosperous, and then thou shalt have good success.

Have not I commanded thee? Be strong and of a good courage; be not afraid, neither be thou dismayed: for the Lord thy God is with thee whithersoever thou goest.   Joshua 1:3, 5, & 8-9

And Joshua fell on his face to the earth and did worship and said, "Thank You, Captain."

Now, take a look with me at one of God's heroes (one of mine as well), the great prophet Elijah. He had obeyed God, seen the fire of God fall, killed four hundred and fifty prophets of Baal, prayed for the rain, outran the fastest horses in Israel. And then he had a message from Queen Jezebel threatening to kill him. He would be as dead as her prophets were, she said.

One moment he was making headlines as, *The Man of the Hour*; the next moment he was an embarrassment to himself and to everyone else. He thought it was just better to die. But God had other thoughts. When He takes His people home, He wants it to be in victory.

And when he saw that, he arose, and went for his life, and came to Beersheba, which belongeth to Judah, and left his servant there. But he himself went a day's journey into the wilderness, and came and sat down under a juniper tree: and he requested for himself that he might die; and said, it is enough; now, O Lord, take away my life; for I am not better than my fathers. And as he lay and slept under a juniper tree, behold, then an angel touched him, and said unto him, Arise and eat. And he looked, and, behold, there was a cake baken on the coals, and a cruse of water at his head. And he did eat and drink, and laid him down again. And the angel of the Lord came again the second time, and touched him, and said, Arise and eat; because the journey is too great for thee. And he arose, and did eat and drink, and went in the strength of that meat forty days and forty nights unto Horeb the mount of God.   I Kings 19:3-8

Elijah was not resting in God. He had rested in his faith in God on Mount Carmel. Now, he slept as a result of depression brought on by fear, not only for his life, but also that he would be humiliated and scorned by his enemy.

When you are depressed, you need a meal of the supernatural Word of God. If you will let Him feed you, the Lord will always do it. He knows what you need; and He has what you need.

God didn't berate Elijah for his weakness and failure. He allowed him to sleep. Then He offered him something to make him stronger, a supernatural meal.

And there was a voice from the firmament that was over their heads: When Ezekiel saw the creatures put their wings down to rest, he also heard a voice from above them. The voice of God comforts the weary soldier. He understands our need to rest. He said to Elijah, "The journey is too great for thee." He calls us to feed and to be restored. He has supernatural strength for us — if we are willing to partake of it.

On the strength of that one meal, Elijah went for *forty days and forty nights unto Horeb the mount of God.* When he got to Horeb, he came to know God in another capacity.

> *And he said, Go forth, and stand upon the mount before the Lord. And, behold, the Lord passed by, and a great and strong wind rent the mountains, and brake in pieces the rocks before the Lord; but the Lord was not in the wind: and after the wind an earthquake; but the Lord was not in the earthquake: And after the earthquake a fire; but the Lord was not in the fire: and after the fire a still small voice. And it was so, when Elijah heard it, that he wrapped his face in his mantle, and went out, and stood in the entering in of the cave. And, behold, there came a voice unto him, and said, What doest thou here, Elijah?* 1 Kings 19:11-13

Some people have limited God. He can only move in the way in which they are accustomed. They only see Him in one particular way. He might be present and working and speaking, but if what they always expect and look for is not happening, they don't receive anything at all.

God is not always in a strong wind. He is not always in an earthquake. He is not always in a fire. Sometimes He is in a still, small voice.

A voice was heard above the living creatures. God was present to restore their strength, to revitalize their spirits.

> *And he said, I have been very jealous for the Lord God of hosts: because the children of Israel have forsaken thy covenant, thrown down thine altars, and slain thy prophets with the sword; and I, even I only, am left; and they seek my life, to take it away.*
>
> 1 Kings 19:14

The Lord did not even respond to this statement. There was work to be done. So He sent Elijah on his way.

> *And the Lord said unto him, Go, return on thy way to the wilderness of Damascus: and when thou comest, anoint Hazael to be king over Syria: And Jehu the son of Nimshi shalt thou anoint to be king over Israel: and Elisha the son of Shaphat of Abelmeholah shalt thou anoint to be prophet in thy room.* 1 Kings 19:15-16

Standing with relaxed wings is not our permanent position. It is only momentary. There is much work to be done. Be refreshed, then get back into battle quickly. Get back to the harvest field quickly. The grain is falling.

We must not allow any circumstance or person to influence us to give up our ministry. The wheels that Ezekiel saw were lifted up over against them; for the spirit of the living creature was in the wheels.

Our life, or the spirit of the living creatures, is in the purposes of God in us. It was not God's will in Elijah's life to take him home in the wilderness. God had a higher calling for him. God had a golden chariot of fire and horses of fire prepared, standing on the alert, for the command to fly God's hero home. Elijah had believed God to send fire to prove Himself to the unbelieving people of Israel, but he had not anticipated that he would be transported by that same fire.

At this moment, Elijah thought he had no future. He only saw the threatening, painted face of Jezebel. But God fed him and led him to the Mount of God.

God has great plans for you! The wheels of God in your life are in you and beside you to fulfill His purposes for you.

The Lord Himself is waiting for the command of His Father. We are destined to hear the shout of Jesus, *the voice of the archangel, the trump of God.* The clouds are waiting to transport us home to be with Jesus forever!   ✱

Chapter XIV

The Living One Speaks

And there was a voice from the firmament that was over their heads, when they stood, and had let down their wings. And above the firmament that was over their heads was the likeness of a throne, as the appearance of a sapphire stone: and upon the likeness of the throne was the likeness as the appearance of a man above upon it. And I saw as the colour of amber, as the appearance of fire round about within it, from the appearance of his loins even upward, and from the appearance of his loins even downward, I saw as it were the appearance of fire, and it had brightness round about.

Ezekiel 1:25-27

What Ezekiel saw is described in detail in the Book of Revelation. Therefore, I will only outline verses twenty-five and twenty-seven and will go into the description of the throne in a later chapter.

I want you to see that there was a voice from the firmament, a voice from Heaven, when the living creatures *stood* and *had let down their wings.* I also want us to see the description of the man that sat upon the throne:

> *and upon the likeness of the throne was the likeness as the appearance of a man above upon it. And I saw as the colour of amber, as the appearance of fire round about within it, from the appearance of his loins even upward, and from the appearance of his loins even downward, I saw as it were the appearance of fire, and it had brightness round about.*

This is a description of the Living One, the Christ in all His beauty, speaking to His Church. His voice came from the firmament over the heads of the living creatures when they had stood still and let down their wings. Often, we are too busy to hear what the Lord is trying to say to us. When we take time from our busy schedule to listen, it is amazing what He has to tell us and astounding what He will show us.

Ezekiel saw *the colour of amber from the appearance of the man's loins upward, and from the appearance of his loins downward* he saw the appearance of fire.

> *And I looked, and, behold, a whirlwind came out of the north, a great cloud, and a fire infolding itself, and a brightness was about it, and out of the midst thereof as the colour of amber, out of the midst of the fire. Also out of the midst thereof came the likeness of four living creatures. And this was their appearance; they had the likeness of a man.*   Ezekiel 1:4-5

Ezekiel saw the phenomenon of Pentecost; and in verses twenty-six and twenty-seven he sees the Baptizer with the Holy Ghost and fire, Jesus Christ. This same description of the Lord is given by Daniel as he sought the Lord some fifty-five years later. He wrote:

> *In the third year of Cyrus king of Persia a thing was revealed unto Daniel, whose name was called Belteshazzar; and the thing was true, but the time appointed was long: and he understood the thing, and had understanding of the vision. In those days I Daniel was*

mourning three full weeks. I ate no pleasant bread, neither came flesh nor wine in my mouth, neither did I anoint myself at all, till three whole weeks were fulfilled. And in the four and twentieth day of the first month, as I was by the side of the great river, which is Hiddekel; Then I lifted up mine eyes, and looked, and behold a certain man clothed in linen, whose loins were girded with fine gold of Uphaz: Daniel 10:1-5

This *certain man* was *clothed in linen.* His loins were *girded with fine gold of Uphaz.* When Ezekiel saw Him, the focal point was His loins. Ezekiel said: *And I saw as the colour of amber, from the appearance of his loins even upward, and from the appearance of his loins even downward, I saw as it were the appearance of fire.*

Girding up the loins denotes preparation for battle or for active exertion. When Ezekiel saw Christ talking to the living creatures from heaven, He was girded with light *(the colour of amber)* in his upward parts above the loins and in fire in his legs and feet. However, his loins were girded with both light and fire.

Daniel saw him with loins girded with *the fine gold of Uphaz,* the finest gold obtainable, the same gold used in Solomon's Temple. No doubt Daniel had to be reminded of the gold of the Temple that had already been destroyed. The One that came to speak to Daniel was girded in that same enduring gold in preparation for His labour in the restoration of the Temple.

Let us lift up our eyes and see the God of Pentecost, girded with the gold of heaven, seated upon His throne and we ourselves with Him.

Daniel continued his description:

His body also was like the Beryl, and his face as the appearance of lightning, and his eyes as lamps of fire, and his arms and his feet like in colour to polished brass, and the voice of his words like the voice of a multitude. Daniel 10:6

God spoke to Daniel, even as He spoke to the living creatures; and Daniel says, *the voice of His words was like the voice of a multitude.* Remember, we are considering especially Ezekiel 1:25: *And there was a voice from the firmament* and a description of the One who spoke.

> *And I Daniel alone saw the vision: for the men that were with me saw not the vision; but a great quaking fell upon them, so that they fled to hide themselves.*   Daniel 10:7

Hearing from the prophets is one thing; but hearing directly from the Lord is quite another. Although most Christians have long ago given up hope of hearing directly from Heaven, God hasn't changed His desire to speak directly to men.

Some people are in a position to see the Lord and hear His voice. When our church services are ended, some leave having seen nothing, while others have seen amazing things. The difference is not with God, but with man. Everyone who is in a position to see a particular revelation will see it. In the natural, we cannot understand things unless we are paying attention and listening well. It is the same in the spiritual realm.

> *Therefore I was left alone, and saw this great vision, and there remained no strength in me: for my comeliness was turned in me into corruption, and I retained no strength.*   Daniel 10:8

The Spirit of God overwhelms the flesh. Those who frequently experience the anointing of the Spirit of God in their lives testify of a similar experience. That anointing drains the fleshly part of you.

> *Yet heard I the voice of his words: and when I heard the voice of his words, then was I in a deep sleep on my face, and my face toward the ground.*   Daniel 10:9

Daniel was actually lost in the Spirit, in a *deep sleep.*

> *And, behold, an hand touched me, which set me upon my knees and upon the palms of my hands.*   Daniel 10:10

Ezekiel had this same experience:

> *... when I saw it, I fell upon my face, and I heard a voice of one that spake.*   Ezekiel 1:28

Behold, an hand touched me.: Daniel saw some of that which would happen to Israel and the nations before the second return of the Messiah.

The word of the Lord came expressly unto Ezekiel the priest ... and the hand of the Lord was there upon him.   Ezekiel 1:4

As the hand of the Lord was upon Ezekiel, he saw Pentecost bringing forth the Body of Jesus Christ. He saw the Word of the Lord in this, his first recorded vision, and Ezekiel the priest became Ezekiel the prophet.

Just as He had touched Daniel on the shoulder, in the same manner as He laid his hand on Ezekiel, Jesus visited John in his exile on the Isle of Patmos.

I was in the Spirit on the Lord's day, and heard behind me a great voice, as of a trumpet,   Revelation 1:10

The Apostle John must have been approximately ninety years of age when he received this revelation. He may have thought he was old enough to retire; but there is no retirement in God. We are never too old to receive the Word of the Lord. Age, in fact, is a blessing. The experience of the years and the accumulated knowledge it brings often help us to understand what God is saying to us.

When the living creatures let down their wings, a voice was heard from heaven. When Daniel sought the Lord for three full weeks, the voice of the Lord came to him *like the voice of a multitude.* Now John, resting *on the Lord's day,* heard a *great voice, as of a trumpet.*

Some people say, "The Lord doesn't need to shout." He doesn't need to, but He does anyway. His is a voice of authority. It is like a trumpet. John continues:

Saying, I am Alpha and Omega, the first and the last: and, What thou seest, write in a book, and send it unto the seven churches which are in Asia; unto Ephesus, and unto Smyrna, and unto

Pergamos, and unto Thyatira, and unto Sardis, and unto Philadel-
phia, and unto Laodicea.   Revelation 1:11

God has a voice; and He can be heard — if we are willing to listen.
God is real; and He can be seen — if we are willing to look for Him.
John listened to the voice. He *turned to see* the voice, the Word which
was from the beginning.

In the beginning was the Word, and the Word was with God, and
the Word was God.   John 1:1

The deepest revelation of all sacred Scripture is found in this word
given to John. Most people have not been able to understand it yet
because God has not revealed it to them. But, little by little, the veil is
being lifted from it.

And I turned to see the voice that spake with me. And being turned,
I saw seven golden candlesticks; And in the midst of the seven
candlesticks one like unto the Son of man, clothed with a garment
down to the foot, and girt about the paps with a golden girdle. His
head and his hairs were white like wool, as white as snow; and his
eyes were as a flame of fire; And his feet like unto fine brass, as if they
burned in a furnace; and his voice as the sound of many waters. And
he had in his right hand seven stars: and out of his mouth went a
sharp twoedged sword: and his countenance was as the sun shineth
in his strength. And when I saw him, I fell at his feet as dead. And he
laid his right hand upon me, saying unto me, Fear not; I am the first
and the last: I am he that liveth, and was dead; and, behold, I am
alive for evermore, Amen; and have the keys of hell and of death.
                                                                                           Revelation 1:12-18

This is the same One that Ezekiel saw, the same One that Daniel was
privileged to see. John's reaction was the same as the others. He fell on
his face.

Ezekiel fell upon his face. Daniel was touched by an invisible hand
that set him upon his knees and upon the palms of his hands. And John
fell at the Lord's feet like a dead man. Notice the similarity of the

description of the Christ that is given to us by Ezekiel, Daniel and John — the glory *(colour of amber)* and the fire. Hallelujah!

God commissioned John, in his old age, to do the greatest work he had ever done and gave him one of the greatest revelations any man has received. What a mighty God we serve!

The message that God gave John for each of the seven churches was different. Each message addressed the personal need of that particular congregation. God meets us where we are. He knows our needs and knows how to address them.

After He had given John the message for each of the seven churches, the revelation continued:

> *After this I looked, and, behold, a door was opened in heaven: and the first voice which I heard was as it were of a trumpet talking with me; which said, Come up hither, and I will shew thee things which must be hereafter. And immediately I was in the spirit: and, behold, a throne was set in heaven, and one sat on the throne. And he that sat was to look upon like a jasper and a sardine stone: and there was a rainbow round about the throne, in sight like unto an emerald.*
>
> Revelation 4:1-3

This is very much the same picture that Ezekiel saw. He said:

> *And above the firmament that was over their heads was the likeness of a throne, as the appearance of a sapphire stone: and upon the likeness of the throne was the likeness as the appearance of a man above upon it. And I saw as the colour of amber, as the appearance of fire round about within it, from the appearance of his loins even upward, and from the appearance of his loins even downward, I saw as it were the appearance of fire, and it had brightness round about. As the appearance of the bow that is in the cloud in the day of rain, so was the appearance of the brightness round about. This was the appearance of the likeness of the glory of the Lord. And when I saw it, I fell upon my face, and I heard a voice of one that spake.*
>
> Ezekiel 1:26-28

And he said unto me, Son of man, stand upon thy feet, and I will speak unto thee. And the spirit entered into me when he spake unto me, and set me upon my feet, that I heard him that spake unto me. And he said unto me, Son of man, I send thee to the children of Israel, to a rebellious nation that hath rebelled against me: they and their fathers have transgressed against me, even unto this very day.

Ezekiel 2:1-3

God gave John a message to the seven churches of Asia Minor. He sent Ezekiel to the rebellious nation of Israel. And God showed Daniel what would happen to Israel in the latter days. His vision was for a future time, *yet for many days.*

Nothing strengthens us like the Word of the Lord. When He comes to us and speaks to us, every weakness takes flight. This Word will stay with you in times of test and trial. Faithful Christians are those who have learned to receive the Word of the Lord, not necessarily those who are most emotional.

Those of us who are dedicated to seeing a mighty move of God in the whole earth in these end times must determine to make the personal word of the Lord for each of our lives a priority. His Word is solid food. And this is what we live on, not on stimulants. His Word is the strength of our lives. Ezekiel said: *And the Spirit entered into me when He spake unto me, and set me upon my feet.*

The Word of God will keep you from becoming depressed or oppressed. It will keep you from running when things get tough. It will place you firmly on the Solid Rock. God told Daniel to *be strong.* I want to shout that out to every Christian who can hear me.

Be strong! Yea, be Strong!

God hasn't changed. We can be strong in Him.

This has nothing to do with our physique. The physique is not nearly as important as the world tries to make it. The condition of your soul is what will determine your future.

God, who at sundry times and in divers manners spake in time past unto the fathers by the prophets, Hath in these last days spoken unto us by his Son, whom he hath appointed heir of all things, by whom also he made the worlds; Hebrews 1:1-2

I want you to notice, however, that the Word of the Lord, whether given through an angel, through a human messenger, or by the Lord Himself, had that strengthening influence.

Paul's prayer for the Ephesians is revealing:

Wherefore I also, after I heard of your faith in the Lord Jesus, and love unto all the saints, Cease not to give thanks for you, making mention of you in my prayers; That the God of our Lord Jesus Christ, the Father of glory, may give unto you the spirit of wisdom and revelation in the knowledge of him: the eyes of your understanding being enlightened; that ye may know what is the hope of his calling, and what the riches of the glory of his inheritance in the saints, And what is the exceeding greatness of his power to us-ward who believe, according to the working of his mighty power, Which he wrought in Christ, when he raised him from the dead, and set him at his own right hand in the heavenly places, Far above all principality, and power, and might, and dominion, and every name that is named, not only in this world, but also in that which is to come: And hath put all things under his feet, and gave him to be the head over all things to the church, Which is his body, the fulness of him that filleth all in all.

And you hath he quickened, who were dead in trespasses and sins; But God, who is rich in mercy, for his great love wherewith he loved us, Even when we were dead in sins, hath quickened us together with Christ, (by grace ye are saved;) And hath raised us up together, and made us sit together in heavenly places in Christ Jesus: That in the ages to come he might shew the exceeding riches of his grace in his kindness toward us through Christ Jesus.

Ephesians 1:15-2:1 & 4-7

God has raised us up by His Word. It was the power of His Word that brought us from spiritual death into the born again experience and made us to *sit in heavenly places.* It was the Word that made us see that we were sinners. It was the Word that made us see that we needed to be saved. It was the Word that made us see that He is the Saviour. And it was the Word that led us to accept Him. Thank God for His Word.

The same Jesus Who spoke to Daniel, to Ezekiel and to John wants to reveal Himself to you personally. You don't have to be a special person to be able to hear Him speak. His desire is that every man and woman know His voice.

You may be a sinner. If so, Jesus loves you. If you will open your heart and mind to Him, He will speak to you and save you. He will show you the wonderful things He is able do with your life and what He can do with you as a person.

If you are already a Christian, God has so much more for you. He wants you to see His Word. He wants to feed you on your particular level of development, then quickly take you to other levels and greater revelation in His Word.

Once you have left the milk stage, you need to begin praying the prayer of Paul that God would *give unto you the spirit of wisdom and revelation in the knowledge of him: the eyes of your understanding being enlightened; that ye may know what is the hope of his calling, and what the riches of the glory of his inheritance in the saints, And what is the exceeding greatness of his power to us-ward who believe.*

Pray thus for one another, and together let us see the glory of God and the revelation of Jesus Christ, the Living One.   �֎

Chapter XV

The Living Stone and the Lively Stones

And there was a voice from the firmament that was over their heads, when they stood, and had let down their wings. And above the firmament that was over their heads was the likeness of a throne, as the appearance of a sapphire stone: and upon the likeness of the throne was the likeness as the appearance of a man above upon it. And I saw as the colour of amber, as the appearance of fire round about within it, from the appearance of his loins even upward, and from the appearance of his loins even downward, I saw as it were the appearance of fire, and it had brightness round about. As the appearance of the bow that is in the cloud in the day of rain, so was the appearance of the brightness round about.   Ezekiel 1:25-28a

This is not the first time God has portrayed Himself as a stone. When Moses went up to the mountain with the other leaders of Israel, they saw God's throne *as the appearance of a sapphire stone.*

*Then went up Moses, and Aaron, Nadab, and Abihu, and seventy of
the elders of Israel: And they saw the God of Israel: and there was
under his feet as it were a paved work of a sapphire stone, and as it
were the body of heaven in his clearness.*   Exodus 24:9-10

John saw the same thing in his revelation.

*After this I looked, and, behold, a door was opened in heaven: and the
first voice which I heard was as it were of a trumpet talking with me;
which said, Come up hither, and I will shew thee things which must
be hereafter. And immediately I was in the spirit: and, behold, a
throne was set in heaven, and one sat on the throne. And he that sat
was to look upon like a jasper and a sardine stone: and there was a
rainbow round about the throne, in sight like unto an emerald.*
                                                        Revelation 4:1-3

Let us compare the records of the prophet Ezekiel and the Apostle
John. They both heard a voice; both saw Christ sitting up a throne and
a rainbow around the throne. The throne, the One who sat upon the
throne, and the rainbow are all seen as stones.

The likeness of a throne: as the appearance of a sapphire stone (Ezekiel 1:26
and Exodus 24:10).

He that sat upon the throne: a jasper and sardine stone (Revelation 4:3).

Rainbow round about the throne: (Revelation 4:3).

Peter saw Christ as *a living stone,* and us, as the creation of God, as
lively stones.

*Wherefore laying aside all malice, and all guile, and hypocrisies, and
envies, and all evil speakings, As newborn babes, desire the sincere
milk of the word, that ye may grow thereby: If so be ye have tasted
that the Lord is gracious. To whom coming, as unto a living stone,
disallowed indeed of men, but chosen of God, and precious, Ye also,
as lively stones, are built up a spiritual house, an holy priesthood, to
offer up spiritual sacrifices, acceptable to God by Jesus Christ.*
                                                        1 Peter 2:1-5

This *living stone* is *precious;* and we are precious in Him. Since we are to be as He is, this is a great motivation to lay aside *all malice, and all guile, and hypocrisies, and envies, and all evil speakings.* Emeralds were not created to be covered with dirt. Nothing could better hide the value and beauty of a real gem than dirt. If a jewel is covered with dust and grime, its beauty is hidden.

Peter is saying, "Please clean yourselves up and see what God has in you." Lay aside all *malice.* Lay aside all *hypocrisies.* Put away all *evil speaking.* Just because something is true doesn't give you the right to talk about it. Put away ALL *evil speaking.*

> *Wherefore also it is contained in the scripture, Behold, I lay in Sion a chief corner stone, elect, precious: and he that believeth on him shall not be confounded. Unto you therefore which believe he is precious: but unto them which be disobedient, the stone which the builders disallowed, the same is made the head of the corner,*
>
> 1 Peter 2:6-7

To those of us who believe, Jesus Christ is precious. The fact that many do not believe doesn't change anything. He is still *the Head of the corner.* Your unbelief doesn't change Him. You are the one who needs changing. My unbelief doesn't change Him. I am the one who needs changing. He doesn't change.

> *And a stone of stumbling, and a rock of offence, even to them which stumble at the word, being disobedient: whereunto also they were appointed. But ye are a chosen generation, a royal priesthood, an holy nation, a peculiar people; that ye should shew forth the praises of him who hath called you out of darkness into his marvellous light;*
>
> 1 Peter 2:8-9

You are *a chosen generation.* You are *a royal priesthood.* You are *an holy nation.* You are God's *peculiar people.* Why? He has ordained you *to show forth the praises of Him who hath called you.*

Someone could give you the most precious diamond in the world, and that diamond would not show forth the praises of him that gave it to you unless you had it cleaned. You could walk around with it, and nobody would even notice it. Nobody would say, "Who gave you that beautiful diamond?" In order to show forth God's praises, you have to be cleaned and polished.

> *Which in time past were not a people, but are now the people of God: which had not obtained mercy, but now have obtained mercy. Dearly beloved, I beseech you as strangers and pilgrims, abstain from fleshly lusts, which war against the soul; Having your conversation honest among the Gentiles: that, whereas they speak against you as evildoers, they may by your good works, which they shall behold, glorify God in the day of visitation. Submit yourselves to every ordinance of man for the Lord's sake: whether it be to the king, as supreme;*   1 Peter 2:10-13

The lusts of the flesh *war against the soul*. We need to die to self. We need to pursue *good works*. In that way, we will *glorify God*.

> *Wherefore come out from among them, and be ye separate, saith the Lord, and touch not the unclean thing; and I will receive you. And will be a Father unto you, and ye shall be my sons and daughters, saith the Lord Almighty. Having therefore these promises, dearly beloved, let us cleanse ourselves from all filthiness of the flesh and spirit, perfecting holiness in the fear of God.*
>   2 Corinthians 6:17-7:1

> *And above the firmament that was over their heads was the likeness of a throne, as the appearance of a sapphire stone: and upon the likeness of the throne was the likeness as the appearance of a man above upon it.*   Ezekiel 1:26

Let's take another look at what Ezekiel saw following his revelation of the living creatures and their ministry, depicting to us the Body of Jesus Christ and our ministry.

Ezekiel saw, over the heads of the living creatures (in the heavenlies), the likeness of a throne that looked *like a sapphire stone*. Then he saw the appearance of a man upon the throne and described the Living One in His glory. Ezekiel saw as *the colour of amber from His loins upward, and from His loins downward,* Ezekiel saw *as the appearance of fire.* There was no diminishing of His glory as it originated in His loins, in the strength of His being.

Ezekiel saw the Christ as a Man. Peter called Him the Living Stone. John said that He *was to look upon like a jasper and a sardine stone.*

The jasper is an opaque variety of quartz iron oxide. The colours of the jasper stone are: white, red, yellow, brown and black, the same as the races of mankind. Jesus identifies with the white race, with the red race, with the yellow race, with the brown race and with the black race.

A second definition of jasper is: *a green, precious stone of ancient times.* He is *the Ancient of Days.* He is the God of all generations. He is Lord of the past, present and future.

He is Royalty of Heaven, come to earth, portraying the colours of the five races of mankind, that we might become the Royalty of heaven, kings and priests unto our God.

He is *as a sardine stone.* The sard or carnelian stone of sardis is a blood red or flesh-coloured stone. This speaks to us of the fact that Jesus became flesh to take upon Himself the sins of mankind. It speaks to us that, by the price of His blood, He purchased all nations. He *became flesh* that we might become divine. Through Him, we become precious stones.

We are emeralds. The emerald is a bright green, precious stone, a transparent green beryl. The beryl's colour is green, with traces of chromium. The emerald is blue-green or aqua-marine. Other emeralds are a bright green variety of chortle or sapphire.

The sardias, probably a blood-red ruby, was the first precious stone in the first row of the High Priest's breastplate. He wore it when he interceded on behalf of the people.

And thou shalt make the breastplate of judgment with cunning work; after the work of the ephod thou shalt make it; of gold, of blue, and of purple, and of scarlet, and of fine twined linen, shalt thou make it. Foursquare it shall be being doubled; a span shall be the length thereof, and a span shall be the breadth thereof. And thou

shalt set in it settings of stones, even four rows of stones: the first row shall be a sardius, a topaz, and a carbuncle: this shall be the first row. And the second row shall be an emerald, a sapphire, and a diamond. And the third row a ligure, an agate, and an amethyst. And the fourth row a beryl, and an onyx, and a jasper: they shall be set in gold in their inclosings. And the stones shall be with the names of the children of Israel, twelve, according to their names, like the engravings of a signet; every one with his name shall they be according to the twelve tribes. And thou shalt make upon the breastplate chains at the ends of wreathen work of pure gold.
                                                    Exodus 28:15-22

Our Lord is said to be *like unto a jasper and sardine stone*. We are with Him on His throne. We are seen as *the emerald*. The emerald is a sapphire, and the throne is *like a sapphire*.

The sardius stone was the first stone on the breastplate of the High Priest, and the jasper was the last. When John saw Jesus Christ, he saw Him *as a jasper and sardine stone*. He is our great High Priest that intercedes on our behalf for all eternity, and on His breastplate all these precious stones can be found. He is likened to the first one *(the sardius)* and to the last one *(the jasper)*.

These stones are also found in the foundations of the city, New Jerusalem.

And the building of the wall of it was of jasper: and the city was pure gold, like unto clear glass. And the foundations of the wall of the city were garnished with all manner of precious stones. The first foundation was jasper; the second, sapphire; the third, a chalcedony; the fourth, an emerald; The fifth, sardonyx; the sixth, sardius; the seventh, chrysolite; the eighth, beryl; the ninth, a topaz; the tenth, a chrysoprasus; the eleventh, a jacinth; the twelfth, an amethyst. And the twelve gates were twelve pearls: every several gate was of one pearl: and the street of the city was pure gold, as it were transparent glass.   Revelation 21:18-21

The first foundation was *jasper*. The sixth was the *sardius*. The *sapphire* was second. The *beryl* was the eighth.

The Levitical priesthood, represented by the twelve stones of the breastplate, was fulfilled in Christ. As the twelve stones also represented the twelve tribes, we are inscribed in Christ, and He is inscribed in us. He represents all the rainbow of variety found in the children of God, heirs of Abraham, Isaac and Jacob.

The final stone was made the first foundation of the New Jerusalem. We are, thus, totally identified with the Living Stone.

The first stone in the High Priest's breastplate was a sardine stone. It is by the blood that we are born again and become priests unto God. There is no other way to come to God but by the blood of Jesus. There was no other way that He could become our Saviour. He had to take upon Himself our flesh and be tried in all the ways as we are. He became our High Priest because He understands us. He was *in all points tempted like as we are.*

> *For we have not an high priest which cannot be touched with the feeling of our infirmities; but was in all points tempted like as we are, yet without sin.* Hebrews 4:15

Through His sacrifice, we can overcome temptation.

> *There hath no temptation taken you but such as is common to man: but God is faithful, who will not suffer you to be tempted above that ye are able; but will with the temptation also make a way to escape, that ye may be able to bear it.* 1 Corinthians 10:13

The sardius, the blood-red and ruby flesh coloured stone, is the foundation stone of our salvation and of our priesthood. Thank You, Jesus! Listen to John, as he describes the glories that await us as *lively stones:*

> *And I saw a new heaven and a new earth: for the first heaven and the first earth were passed away; and there was no more sea. And I John saw the holy city, new Jerusalem, coming down from God out of heaven, prepared as a bride adorned for her husband. And I heard a great voice out of heaven saying, Behold, the tabernacle of God is*

with men, and he will dwell with them, and they shall be his people, and God himself shall be with them, and be their God. And God shall wipe away all tears from their eyes; and there shall be no more death, neither sorrow, nor crying, neither shall there be any more pain: for the former things are passed away.

And he that sat upon the throne said, Behold, I make all things new. And he said unto me, Write: for these words are true and faithful. And he said unto me, It is done. I am Alpha and Omega, the beginning and the end. I will give unto him that is athirst of the fountain of the water of life freely. He that overcometh shall inherit all things; and I will be his God, and he shall be my son. But the fearful, and unbelieving, and abominable, and murderers, and whoremongers, and sorcerers, and idolaters, and all liars, shall have their part in the lake which burneth with fire and brimstone: which is the second death.

And there came unto me one of the seven angels which had the seven vials full of the seven last plagues, and talked with me, saying, Come hither, I will shew thee the bride, the Lamb's wife.

And he carried me away in the spirit to a great and high mountain, and shewed me that great city, the holy Jerusalem, descending out of heaven from God, Having the glory of God: and her light was like unto a stone most precious, even like a jasper stone, clear as crystal; And had a wall great and high, and had twelve gates, and at the gates twelve angels, and names written thereon, which are the names of the twelve tribes of the children of Israel:

And the wall of the city had twelve foundations, and in them the names of the twelve apostles of the Lamb.

Revelation 21:1-12 & 14

These stones speak of the Christ. *Her light was like unto a stone most precious, even like a jasper stone.* John saw Him *as a jasper and sardine stone.* In the High Priest's breastplate, the sardine stone came first and the jasper stone last. In the foundation of the New Jerusalem, the jasper stone was first. Who is John seeing here? He is not seeing Christ. He is seeing the Bride of Christ, *the Lamb's wife.*

And the building of the wall of it [the New Jerusalem] was of jasper: and the city was pure gold, like unto clear glass.

Revelation 21:18

The Lamb is the light of the New Jerusalem. His light was *like the jasper stone.* He is the Light. He shines in us and makes us shine out His love to a dark world.

Let your light so shine before men, that they may see your good works, and glorify your Father which is in heaven.

Matthew 5:16

We shine forth His light. The Lamb's Bride is like the Lamb. He is the *Living Stone,* and we are *lively stones.*

The building of the wall was of jasper; and the first foundation was *jasper* (see Revelation 21:18-19).

For we are labourers together with God: ye are God's husbandry, ye are God's building. According to the grace of God which is given unto me, as a wise masterbuilder, I have laid the foundation, and another buildeth thereon. But let every man take heed how he buildeth thereupon. For other foundation can no man lay than that is laid, which is Jesus Christ.   1 Corinthians 3:9-11

The first foundation was of jasper. There is no other foundation than Jesus Christ. He is pictured *as a jasper stone,* the One that sits upon the throne. The entire wall, although it has twelve foundations, is said to be *of jasper.* Glory to God! The twelve foundations are different, and yet they are the same.

Paul says exactly the same thing. He says, *"We are labourers together with God — we are God's building."* Paul was given grace as a wise masterbuilder. He said, "I have laid the foundation of jasper (there is no other foundation but Jesus Christ)." "And," He said, *Take heed how you build on that foundation.* What is built on the foundation must be of equal quality. It must be Christ-like. It must be of purest content. The first foundation is of jasper, so the building of the wall must be of jasper too.

Every foundation is different, but the building of every foundation is the same. Christ is all in all. He is the first foundation, and He is in the building of every foundation. He is the work of the building of every foundation.

Why spend our time in carnal things that will be burned up by fire? Why not spend our time laying a good foundation?

> *Now if any man build upon this foundation gold, silver, precious stones, wood, hay, stubble; Every man's work shall be made manifest: for the day shall declare it, because it shall be revealed by fire; and the fire shall try every man's work of what sort it is. If any man's work abide which he hath built thereupon, he shall receive a reward. If any man's work shall be burned, he shall suffer loss: but he himself shall be saved; yet so as by fire. Know ye not that ye are the temple of God, and that the Spirit of God dwelleth in you? If any man defile the temple of God, him shall God destroy; for the temple of God is holy, which temple ye are.*   1 Corinthians 3:12-17

We must first lay a proper foundation, Christ. Then we must take heed how we build on that foundation. We are building a marvellous building. Let us see it as God sees it. Let us be inspired to build well.

It makes my heart sad when I see Christians who are not taking every opportunity to build in their inner man the nature of Christ by the Word of the Living God. When God reveals His Word to you, this is what He is doing. He is building something beautiful in your life. Recognize it and receive it joyfully.

> *To him that overcometh will I grant to sit with me in my throne, even as I also overcame, and am set down with my Father in his throne.*   Revelation 3:21

We are going to sit *in* God's throne. He didn't say "on", as we might have expected. In the preceding verse, He said:

Behold, I stand at the door, and knock: if any man hear my voice, and open the door, I will come in to him, and will sup with him, and he with me. Revelation 3:20

What is God talking about? He is talking about coming into your heart and revealing to you His Word. He wants to give you a banquet of His goodness, by allowing you to eat of His Word. Peter instructed us to drink the milk of the Word, as newborn babes.

As newborn babes, desire the sincere milk of the word, that ye may grow thereby: 1 Peter 2:2

There comes a time, however, when milk is not enough. Then we need the meat of the Word. Jesus wants to come into our lives. He wants to cause us to feast on His Word. He wants to build in us a sure foundation. *Line upon line and precept upon precept,* He wants to establish us and make us overcomers so that we can sit with Him in His throne.

The Saviour of all races of mankind is *as the jasper stone* and *as the sardine stone.* He shed His blood and took upon Himself the flesh of man so that we might become the *lively stones* of God.

Saints of God, may this knowledge encourage you to repent of any hidden sins that may exist in your life so that you may be *the building of the wall,* part of *the Lamb's wife.* Let there be no defilement in God's building. There is no *hay, wood or stubble* in God's wall. These materials must all be burnt up. What remains must be *gold and silver and precious stones.*

May God grant to you that you be a faithful masterbuilder, to lay only the pure foundations of precious stones and to build upon that pure foundation with only the finest and purest materials the *Christ in you, the hope of glory!* ✸

Chapter XVI

The Rainbow

And above the firmament that was over their heads was the likeness of a throne, as the appearance of a sapphire stone: and upon the likeness of the throne was the likeness as the appearance of a man above upon it. And I saw as the colour of amber, as the appearance of fire round about within it, from the appearance of his loins even upward, and from the appearance of his loins even downward, I saw as it were the appearance of fire, and it had brightness round about. As the appearance of the bow that is in the cloud in the day of rain, so was the appearance of the brightness round about. This was the appearance of the likeness of the glory of the Lord. And when I saw it, I fell upon my face, and I heard a voice of one that spake.

Ezekiel 1:26-28

Surely you have seen a rainbow, but have you seen a rainbow that caused you to fall on your face? The impact of the rainbow that Ezekiel saw not only caused him to fall on his face, but also caused him to hear the voice of God — in a life-changing message for this priest in captivity. May this also be your experience, as you see the rainbow that Ezekiel saw.

And when I saw it, I fell upon my face, and I heard a voice of one that spake.   Ezekiel 1:28

And he said unto me, Son of man, I send thee to the children of Israel, to a rebellious nation that hath rebelled against me: they and their fathers have transgressed against me, even unto this very day.
                                                                          Ezekiel 2:3

Ezekiel was commissioned to minister to his own people, but his prophecy that God gave him covers a period that continues to the time of the millennial reign of Christ.

Behold, I have made thy face strong against their faces, and thy forehead strong against their foreheads. As an adamant harder than flint have I made thy forehead: fear them not, neither be dismayed at their looks, though they be a rebellious house.
Then the spirit took me up, and I heard behind me a voice of a great rushing, saying, Blessed be the glory of the Lord from his place. I heard also the noise of the wings of the living creatures that touched one another, and the noise of the wheels over against them, and a noise of a great rushing. So the spirit lifted me up, and took me away, and I went in bitterness, in the heat of my spirit; but the hand of the Lord was strong upon me.   Ezekiel 3:8-9 & 12-14

Ezekiel became that which he saw in the vision — the faces of the living creatures, the lion-like forehead, as he was empowered by the Holy Ghost. God creates in us, by His Spirit, that which we see in His Word. Ezekiel saw the vision, ate God's Word, and began to minister, as God commissioned him. And *the hand of the Lord was* strong *upon him.*

This book has been dedicated to sharing some of the revelation of the first recorded vision that God showed Ezekiel, the priest, as he sat with other captives by the River Chebar. The vision of the living creatures was the springboard of the ministry that God wanted to do through Him.

The "seeing" of this vision is the launching pad that God has used for those who see themselves as *the living creatures* and experience the intent of God in sharing the vision with them, as He did with Ezekiel.

Let us look again at Ezekiel 1:4:

> *And I looked, and, behold, a whirlwind came out of the north, a great cloud, and a fire infolding itself, and a brightness was about it.*

Ezekiel saw Pentecost (whirlwind, cloud, fire) and surrounding this phenomenon was a brightness that Ezekiel does not explain until he sees the Living One on the throne.

> *And above the firmament that was over their heads was the likeness of a throne, as the appearance of a sapphire stone: and upon the likeness of the throne was the likeness as the appearance of a man above upon it. And I saw as the colour of amber, as the appearance of fire round about within it, from the appearance of his loins even upward, and from the appearance of his loins even downward, I saw as it were the appearance of fire, and it had brightness round about.*
>
> Ezekiel 1:26-27

Notice, in verse four, that Ezekiel had seen *a fire enfolding itself*. He said of that fire: *A brightness was about it.* The fire, in this case, was the Christ, the Baptizer with the Holy Ghost. There is a brightness round about that mighty infilling with the Holy Ghost and fire. In verses twenty-six and twenty-seven, Ezekiel saw the Christ, the Baptizer with the Holy Ghost and fire as a Man sitting upon a throne that had *the appearance as a sapphire stone.*

Jesus said to His disciples:

> *Nevertheless I tell you the truth; It is expedient for you that I go away: for if I go not away, the Comforter will not come unto you; but if I depart, I will send him unto you. And when he is come, he will*

reprove the world of sin, and of righteousness, and of judgment: Of sin, because they believe not on me; Of righteousness, because I go to my Father, and ye see me no more; Of judgment, because the prince of this world is judged.   John 16:7-11

And from the appearance of His loins even downward, I saw as it were the appearance of fire, and it had brightness round about: We must now see that this *brightness* not only surrounds an experience of being baptized with the Holy Ghost, but actually surrounds Christ as the Baptizer as He sits upon the throne.

Then Ezekiel describes *the appearance of the brightness round about.* He says that it is: *as the appearance of the bow that is in the cloud in the day of rain.* In other words, the brightness round about the Lord Jesus Christ looks like a rainbow. Ezekiel goes on to say what this rainbow was: *This was the appearance of the likeness of the glory of the Lord.* He didn't say, "This was the appearance of the glory of the Lord," which would have conveyed to us the understanding that the glory of God which surrounded the throne looked like a rainbow.

Ezekiel said: *This* [the brightness round about] *was the appearance of the likeness of the glory of the Lord.* Ezekiel's vision began by his seeing the likeness of four living creatures coming out from the fire of Pentecost (Ezekiel 1:5). The living creatures portray the Christ; and the likeness of the four living creatures portray the Christ-like ones.

Now, Ezekiel sees Christ sitting upon the throne with *the appearance of a sapphire stone* and *as the colour of amber. From the appearance of his loins even upward, and from the appearance of his loins even downward, I saw as it were the appearance of fire, and it had brightness round about.* Again, as Christ sits on His throne, there is a brightness about Him.

This brightness was *as the appearance of the bow that is in the cloud in the day of rain, so was the appearance of the brightness round about.* The brightness around Christ looked like a rainbow.

Before God quickened my vision and my understanding, I thought that Ezekiel had seen what the glory of the Lord was like. God showed me that it is exactly as He said. This was *the appearance of the likeness of the glory of the Lord.*

Just as we are born again into the likeness of Jesus Christ, we are the likeness of the glory of the Lord. To God, we look like a rainbow. This is an enlightening revelation. Hear Jesus praying in the Garden of Gethsemane before He was crucified:

And the glory which thou gavest me I have given them; that they may be one, even as we are one: John 17:22

And then listen to John as he writes to the Church, the likeness of the living creatures:

Beloved, now are we the sons of God, and it doth not yet appear what we shall be: but we know that, when he shall appear, we shall be like him; for we shall see him as he is.   1 John 3:2

John was able to record Jesus' prayer in the garden because he was there praying with Him. He then encouraged the Church to be an answer to the prayer of Jesus; and now God shows John the fulfilment of that prayer in heaven.

After this I looked, and, behold, a door was opened in heaven: and the first voice which I heard was as it were of a trumpet talking with me; which said, Come up hither, and I will shew thee things which must be hereafter. And immediately I was in the spirit: and, behold, a throne was set in heaven, and one sat on the throne. And he that sat was to look upon like a jasper and a sardine stone: and there was a rainbow round about the throne, in sight like unto an emerald.
                                                          Revelation 4:1-3

John saw the same vision that Ezekiel saw — a throne (*as a sapphire stone*) in heaven. The One who sits on the throne looked *like a jasper and sardine stone*. And then John saw *a rainbow round about the throne in sight like an emerald*. This rainbow is identified with the twenty-four elders and *the four beasts full of eyes before and behind*.

And round about the throne were four and twenty seats: and upon the seats I saw four and twenty elders sitting, clothed in white raiment; and they had on their heads crowns of gold.

And before the throne there was a sea of glass like unto crystal: and in the midst of the throne, and round about the throne, were four beasts full of eyes before and behind. And the first beast was like a lion, and the second beast like a calf, and the third beast had a face as a man, and the fourth beast was like a flying eagle. And the four beasts had each of them six wings about him; and they were full of eyes within: and they rest not day and night, saying, Holy, holy, holy, Lord God Almighty, which was, and is, and is to come.

Revelation 4:4 & 6-8

These beasts are the same living creatures that Ezekiel saw in his vision.

And he that sat was to look upon like a jasper and a sardine stone: and there was a rainbow round about the throne, in sight like unto an emerald.   Revelation 4:3

We are the rainbow, but He that sits on the throne is *as a jasper and a sardine stone*. Remember that the jasper stone exists in all the five colours of the races: black, brown, red, yellow and white; also, that the sardine stone is a flesh-coloured stone. Jesus is indentifying Himself with us, as He sits upon His throne that has *the appearance of the sapphire stone*. We, then, are likened to an emerald as John sees *the rainbow in sight like an emerald.*

The sapphire stone which Ezekiel saw in his vision is a transparent blue and speaks of heavenly places. He is heavenly and makes us heavenly also, for the emerald is a type of sapphire.

The dictionary says of sapphire:

A bright, blue, precious stone that is hard and clear (or transparent) like a diamond. A transparent gem. The best known variety of sapphire has a blue tinge caused by impurities of iron and titanuim, but sapphire exists in all colours of the rainbow. The coloured varieties are known as fancy sapphires, except the red gems, which are known as rubies.

Isn't that amazing! We are God's rainbow *(like an emerald)* and His throne is a sapphire (an emerald is one type of sapphire). We are identified as sitting with Him in His throne. We are rulers *together with God.* He has given us dominion over the earth. We have the authority of His power.

An emerald is a type of sapphire. The sapphire can be found in all the colours of the rainbow. As the members of the Body of Christ, with all our variety, we are identified with the throne of God.

This rainbow that John saw was *in sight like unto an emerald.* The reason we are seen as a rainbow that looks like an emerald is that we are still on the earth. Spiritually, we *sit with Christ in heavenly places,* but we are still living upon the earth. The emerald represents the green of the earth.

The rainbow was given by God to Noah as a token, or sign. He had emerged from the Ark, after having come through the Great Flood.

And God spake unto Noah, and to his sons with him, saying, And I, behold, I establish my covenant with you, and with your seed after you; And with every living creature that is with you, of the fowl, of the cattle, and of every beast of the earth with you; from all that go out of the ark, to every beast of the earth. And I will establish my covenant with you, neither shall all flesh be cut off any more by the waters of a flood; neither shall there any more be a flood to destroy the earth. And God said, This is the token of the covenant which I make between me and you and every living creature that is with you, for perpetual generations: I do set my bow in the cloud, and it shall be for a token of a covenant between me and the earth. And it shall come to pass, when I bring a cloud over the earth, that the bow shall be seen in the cloud: And I will remember my covenant, which is between me and you and every living creature of all flesh; and the waters shall no more become a flood to destroy all flesh. And the bow shall be in the cloud; and I will look upon it, that I may remember the everlasting covenant between God and every living creature of all flesh that is upon the earth. And God said unto Noah, This is the token of the covenant, which I have established between me and all flesh that is upon the earth.   Genesis 9:8-17

This is God's covenant with mankind. Every time we see a rainbow, we should remember that God will never again destroy the whole earth by flood. God has never forgotten that promise.

The most beautiful and complete rainbow I ever saw was in Hammerdal in northern Sweden, where I was visiting my niece. It was perfect in its seven colours, and it stretched from horizon to horizon — the most beautiful sight I have ever seen. It seemed to last forever. It dawned on me that I should take a picture of this beautiful rainbow, but it was impossible to get it all in because it was so vast. I do not believe that there is a "spiritual camera" on earth big enough to portray the vastness of God's sign, the Church in the heavens. What a wonderful sign God has given us to be in the heavens!

What does it take to make a rainbow? It takes clouds, rain and sunlight. In this portrayal given to Ezekiel, we see the combination of the sun (Christ, the Sun of Righteousness), the cloud (the Holy Ghost) and the sun shining through the rain (the rain of the Holy Ghost).

Christ is in us. He sits on the throne of our lives. He has made us the brightness round about Him. You may not feel very bright at times. When that happens, you need to start seeing as He sees, knowing as He knows, and understanding as He understands. To Him, you are like a rainbow on a cloudy day.

But to have a rainbow, you have to have the rain. It is not enough to be baptized with the Holy Ghost and leave it at that. We need the constant rain of the Spirit in our lives. Then, when the Son of Righteousness shines through the rain, we appear as rainbows.

Be glad then, ye children of Zion, and rejoice in the Lord your God: for he hath given you the former rain moderately, and he will cause to come down for you the rain, the former rain, and the latter rain in the first month. And the floors shall be full of wheat, and the fats shall overflow with wine and oil.   Joel 2:23-24

Saints of God, let us not grow weary of looking to God for rain. We need it. Without the rain, there is no rainbow. Malachi said:

> For, behold, the day cometh, that shall burn as an oven; and all the proud, yea, and all that do wickedly, shall be stubble: and the day that cometh shall burn them up, saith the Lord of hosts, that it shall leave them neither root nor branch. But unto you that fear my name shall the sun of righteousness arise with healing in his wings; and ye shall go forth, and grow up as calves of the stall. And ye shall tread down the wicked; for they shall be ashes under the soles of your feet in the day that I shall do this, saith the Lord of hosts.
>
> Malachi 4:1-3

God help me to allow the Sun of Righteousness to arise with healing in His wings and shine through the rain of the Holy Ghost in me, in order that I might *grow up in Jesus Christ* in that fullness of His stature that will bring forth His signs and wonders (rainbow) to my generation.

The most important thing that Malachi says here is: *unto you that fear my name shall the sun of righteousness arise with healing in his wings.* The One who shines through us is righteous. He is the Sun of Righteousness. I am convinced that in the days to come God will no longer permit those who are not living in righteousness to continue in the ministry. He is the Sun of Righteousness. He is arising. He expects His people to arise in righteousness as well.

The force that draws people to God is an attraction to the Christ, not an attraction to man. The centre of the universe is the sun, not one of the other planets. And the centre of our spiritual universe is the Sun of Righteousness.

The Gospel shines *in our hearts*. It causes a rainbow to come forth. It gives us *"the light of the knowledge of the glory of God in the face of Jesus Christ"* (2 Corinthians 4:6). This comes about through the engrafting of the Word of God in our hearts.

Paul declares that the *"power"* we have is *"of God, and not of us"* (2 Corinthians 4:7). God has given us the privilege of having that power shine through us to reveal His glory. To Him, we look like a rainbow. We are here to represent God's covenant with the earth.

When Jesus prayed in the Garden of Gethsemane, He spoke of the covenant the Father made with us:

> *For I have given unto them the words which thou gavest me; and they have received them, and have known surely that I came out from thee, and they have believed that thou didst send me. I pray for them: I pray not for the world, but for them which thou hast given me; for they are thine. And all mine are thine, and thine are mine; and I am glorified in them. And now I am no more in the world, but these are in the world, and I come to thee. Holy Father, keep through thine own name those whom thou hast given me, that they may be one, as we are.*   John 17:8-11

Even though we are still in the world, we are precious in His sight. He is *glorified* in us. We are His rainbow.

> *I pray not that thou shouldest take them out of the world, but that thou shouldest keep them from the evil. They are not of the world, even as I am not of the world. Sanctify them through thy truth: thy word is truth. As thou hast sent me into the world, even so have I also sent them into the world. And for their sakes I sanctify myself, that they also might be sanctified through the truth. Neither pray I for these alone, but for them also which shall believe on me through their word; That they all may be one; as thou, Father, art in me, and I in thee, that they also may be one in us: that the world may believe that thou hast sent me.*   John 17:15-21

The same John that recorded the prayer of Jesus in the Garden of Gethsemane saw the answer to that prayer as a door was opened to him in heaven.

> *And he that sat was to look upon like a jasper and a sardine stone: and there was a rainbow round about the throne, in sight like unto an emerald.*   Revelation 4:3

John saw Jesus *as a sardine stone* sitting upon His throne. The sardine stone is found in the five colours of His creation, the human race: black, brown, red, yellow and white. Around God's throne John saw a rainbow, which has seven colours: violet, indigo (blue-violet), blue, green, yellow, orange and red.

Sunlight is actually a combination of these seven colours; and the sunlight is seen in the beauty of the rainbow as it shines through drops of rain. Hallelujah!

The Sun Of Righteousness can be seen in all His beauty (seven is God's number of perfection) in the rainbow, which is actually *the living creatures.*

Furthermore, the colours of the rainbow blend into each other, so that usually the observer can only see four or five colours clearly. Let us blend together *that we may be one* even as the Father and Jesus are one.

If the rain is heavy, the bow may spread all the way across the sky, and its two ends seem to rest on the earth (like the rainbow I saw in my native land, Sweden).

Let there be such a downpour of the Holy Ghost rain that the whole earth shall be filled with His glory. May I see Jesus' prayer in Gethsemane answered through me. A rainbow reaches around the world.

Jesus was praying for us that we might be a sign to the world, that they might believe on Him. We are God's token to our generation. We are His witnesses.

And the glory which thou gavest me I have given them; that they may be one, even as we are one: I in them, and thou in me, that they may be made perfect in one; and that the world may know that thou hast sent me, and hast loved them, as thou hast loved me. Father, I will that they also, whom thou hast given me, be with me where I am; that they may behold my glory, which thou hast given me: for thou lovedst me before the foundation of the world. O righteous Father, the world hath not known thee: but I have known thee, and these have known that thou hast sent me. And I have declared unto them thy name, and will declare it: that the love wherewith thou hast loved me may be in them, and I in them. John 17:22-26

We have the privilege of bearing the glory of the Lord in this world. He has given us His glory. We are the fulfilment of the prayer of Jesus in the garden. We are God's sign to the world. We are His rainbow.

We all believe that God loved His Son, but not many of us believe that God loves us, as He loves His Son. Yet it is true.

For God so loved the world, that he gave his only begotten Son, that whosoever believeth in him should not perish, but have everlasting life.   John 3:16

Here we have the tremendous covenant that Jesus Christ made with His father on behalf of mankind, the covenant by which you and I are signs to this world. We are signs of the glory of God that was given to His Son, for we are *the likeness* of the glory of the Lord.

We are being *"changed into the same image from glory to glory"* (2 Corinthians 3:18). When we look into the Word of God, we see the face of Jesus Christ. We see His image. Then, we are *changed from glory to glory* into the same image.

As we have seen in John's letters to the churches, the person who has the hope of looking like the Lord purifies himself to that end (see I John 3:3). We do not purify ourselves by measuring ourselves among ourselves. We purify ourselves by measuring ourselves with Jesus Christ. We have a long way to go, don't we? We must not stop the purifying process.

We are saved by faith. We are guaranteed an entrance into heaven by the grace of God. And we will accomplish it by assimilating the image of Jesus Christ into our very being, by purifying ourselves as He is pure, by allowing God to work in us, by allowing the Sun of Righteousness to shine forth through us.

What are the colours that are seen in a rainbow? They are all the colours of the spectrum, the colours of light, the colours of the sun. As the rain of the Holy Ghost falls on us and the light of Jesus shines through us, we see the likeness of the glory of the Lord all around us. It is like great, golden rain drops. His beauty is shining through us.

This rainbow is made up of all colours. It includes the black, the brown, the red, the yellow, the white and all the other colours in between. God hasn't excluded any of the races from His glory.

In these days, God is baptizing many born again believers of every denomination, of every race, and of every tongue in the glory of the cloud of His Spirit. In this way, His rainbow is being formed across the earth. People everywhere are searching for truth. They are hungry for reality. They are eager to know God. We, therefore, must be His sign, His token to all humanity, that His love is real and available to *whosoever will.*

But in order for this to happen, among peoples of all races, we need rain. The rainbow is not seen in all its splendour for lack of rain. According to Joel, that much-needed rain will come only through prayer and fasting and seeking the face of God. He promises that God will send rain, *the former and latter rains combined, in the first month* — when His people earnestly seek His face.

In the Jewish calendar, the first month of the year is April. It was April when Jesus knelt in the Garden of Gethsemane and made that covenant with the Father. Through His sacrifice, the process of our redemption began. Before long, with the outpouring of the Spirit upon the lives of the believers, rain began to fall. It was as Jesus had predicted. *Signs* began to follow *them that believe*[d]. Jesus was faithful to His covenant. He promised never to leave us or forsake us, and He has kept that word. He is with us. He works with us, *confirming the word with signs following.*

Until we recognize our true position in Jesus Christ, we can never really know our true potential. God wants to make us see who we are and what we are. We are the children of the living God. His power is within us. We can do anything — through Him. We can suffer anything. We can forsake anything. We can overcome anything.

Catch a glimpse of your true value. Look at yourself as He sees you. Know that you are His rainbow to the world. There could be no greater motivation for world evangelism. We are a sign to the whole earth. From this day forward, let the glory of the Lord be manifested in and through your life, so that the world can behold His likeness and believe. Amen! ✤

Chapter XVII

A Comparison Of the Revelations Given To Ezekiel and To John

After this I looked, and, behold, a door was opened in heaven: and the first voice which I heard was as it were of a trumpet talking with me; which said, Come up hither, and I will shew thee things which must be hereafter. And immediately I was in the spirit: and, behold, a throne was set in heaven, and one sat on the throne. And he that sat was to look upon like a jasper and a sardine stone: and there was a rainbow round about the throne, in sight like unto an emerald. And round about the throne were four and twenty seats: and upon the seats I saw four and twenty elders sitting, clothed in white raiment; and they had on their heads crowns of gold. And out of the throne proceeded lightnings and thunderings and voices: and there were seven lamps of fire burning before the throne, which are the seven Spirits of God. And before the throne there was a sea of glass like unto crystal: and in the midst of the throne, and round about the throne, were four beasts full of eyes before and behind. And the first beast was like a lion, and the second beast like a calf, and the third beast had a face as a man, and the fourth beast was like a flying eagle. And the four beasts had each of them six wings about him; and they were full of eyes within: and they rest not day and night, saying, Holy, holy, holy, Lord God Almighty, which was, and is, and is to come. And when those beasts give glory and honour and thanks to him that sat on the throne, who liveth for ever and ever, The four and twenty elders fall down before him that sat on the throne, and worship him that liveth for ever and ever, and cast their crowns before the throne, saying, Thou art worthy, O Lord, to receive glory and honour and power: for thou hast created all things, and for thy pleasure they are and were created. Revelation 4:9-11

In his revelation, John saw many of the same things Ezekiel was privileged to witness — giving New Testament confirmation to the truths revealed by the Old Testament prophet. There are, however, some important differences that should be noted.

The Living Creatures and Their Faces In John's Revelation

... and in the midst of the throne, and round about the throne, were four beasts full of eyes before and behind. And the first beast was like a lion, and the second beast like a calf, and the third beast had a face as a man, and the fourth beast was like a flying eagle.
Revelation 4:6-7

The living creatures that Ezekiel saw are the same as *the beasts* that John saw. The description of the four beasts makes that fact very clear. The first was *like a lion*. The second was *like a calf*. The third *had a face as a man*. And the fourth was *like a flying eagle*.

Aside from the fact that the ox is now described as *a calf*, there is another basic difference. The first creature no longer has the face of a lion. It is now *like a lion*. This is a big difference. The work that God has begun in each of His children will be completed. The image which He has begun to form in us, by the action of the Spirit and the Word, will be finished. We will become like lions.

Let me remind you that lions are not afraid of anything and don't worry about anything. They don't run away from danger. They stand boldly and face any predator.

Let us give Satan notice. We are becoming lions in God. God let John see the finished product, and it was glorious.

The creature with the face of an *ox* has now become *like a calf.* The humility of Christ is being engrafted into us day by day, until soon we shall be like Him in every way. When we stand before His throne, it will not be with earth's pride, but with heaven's humility.

For the moment, let us skip the third beast.

The fourth creature, who once bore the resemblance of an eagle, is now *like a flying eagle.* God knows the beginning from the end. He knows what has been, what is, and what will be. And He sees us flying. That excites me. He is encouraging us to get off the ground. Our end is a glorious one. Don't stay earth-bound any longer. Get started flying.

Sometimes we get weary and feel that we cannot go on. Long ago, Isaiah received a word from God for His weary children:

> *Hast thou not known? hast thou not heard, that the everlasting God, the Lord, the Creator of the ends of the earth, fainteth not, neither is weary? there is no searching of his understanding. He giveth power to the faint; and to them that have no might he increaseth strength. Even the youths shall faint and be weary, and the young men shall utterly fall: But they that wait upon the Lord shall renew their strength; they shall mount up with wings as eagles; they shall run, and not be weary; and they shall walk, and not faint.*
>
> Isaiah 40:28-31

He is speaking *to them that have no might.* Many of us can identify with this passage. We know what it is to run out of steam. Even young people get tired. But there is hope. God is willing to increase our strength.

He is asking one thing: that we *wait upon* Him. May God help me to be a waitress that He can depend on to do His bidding and fulfil His orders no matter how I feel; realizing that He who lives in me *fainteth not neither is weary.* May we, as waiters and waitresses, be always at His side to serve our Creator, and He will do all that He has promised us. His promise is that we *shall renew* [our] *strength, that we shall mount up with wings as eagles, that we shall run, and not be weary,* that we shall *walk, and not faint.* What wonderful promises!

Take wing, my brothers and sisters. You are destined to soar, and God foresees you attaining your final destiny.

Why did the third creature, whom Ezekiel saw with *the face of man,* still have the face of a man when John saw him? I can only surmise that this is another man. Jesus Christ took upon Himself the likeness of carnal flesh, the likeness of man. Since, in every other way, we are like Him in John's revelation, I can only suppose that this is the image of the Man which John sees upon us. We will be Christ-like. Our destiny is clear. As John said to the churches in his letter, *"We shall be like Him"* (1 John 3:2).

Although we have not yet arrived at perfection in Christ, God hasn't finished with us yet. Bit by bit, and piece by piece, He is working out His glorious will in our lives.

The Wings and the Hands Of A Man In John's Revelation

> *And the four beasts had each of them six wings about him; and they were full of eyes within: and they rest not day and night, saying, Holy, holy, holy, Lord God Almighty, which was, and is, and is to come. And when those beasts give glory and honour and thanks to him that sat on the throne, who liveth for ever and ever,*
> Revelation 4:8-9

John saw the four beasts with six wings each, while Ezekiel saw the living creatures with four wings each and two hands. Both saw us as heavenly creatures, but John saw us at a stage where we no longer need earthly hands. The hands were replaced by two more wings. Now, we have a dual role to fulfil, an earthly role and a heavenly role.

> *Verily I say unto you, Whatsoever ye shall bind on earth shall be bound in heaven: and whatsoever ye shall loose on earth shall be loosed in heaven. Again I say unto you, That if two of you shall*

agree on earth as touching any thing that they shall ask, it shall be done for them of my Father which is in heaven. For where two or three are gathered together in my name, there am I in the midst of them.   Matthew 18:18-20

God has linked us with His heavenly authority and with His heavenly glory by His very purpose in us and by His call upon our lives. I believe in the prayer He prayed. I am sure He did not pray it in vain. We will be *sanctified through the truth.* We will become *one ... that the world may believe.* Just as the living creatures were joined by their wings, we will be joined by the action of the glory of God in our lives. We will learn to *walk worthy of God.*

That ye would walk worthy of God, who hath called you unto his kingdom and glory. For this cause also thank we God without ceasing, because, when ye received the word of God which ye heard of us, ye received it not as the word of men, but as it is in truth, the word of God, which effectually worketh also in you that believe.
                                        1 Thessalonians 2:12-13

We can enter God's kingdom and glory now, as a foretaste of that glorious inheritance that we will have for all eternity. Someday we will have no more need of the earthly.

John saw the beasts praising God, just as Ezekiel had seen them with their wings upraised. The beasts *rest not day or night* from their praise. They *give glory and honour and thanks to Him that* sits *on the throne.* What a privilege is ours, that of praising our God, Who lives *for ever and ever!* We will no longer grow weary. Therefore, we will never need to rest.

Jesus Christ In the Midst Of the Churches In John's Revelation

And in the midst of the seven candlesticks one like unto the Son of man, clothed with a garment down to the foot, and girt about the paps with a golden girdle. His head and his hairs were white like wool, as white as snow; and his eyes were as a flame of fire; And his feet like unto fine brass, as if they burned in a furnace; and his voice as the sound of many waters.   Revelation 1:13-15

Just as Ezekiel saw the Lord Jesus Christ in the midst of the churches, John witnessed the Lord *in the midst of the seven golden candlesticks.* And the description of the man John saw is the same as the man Ezekiel saw. Jesus walks with me as a man. His presence is so real. To me personally, He has always revealed His presence on my right side. Whether He was walking with me down the street, standing beside me in my bedroom, with me in the car park, or on the platform in church, He has always been at my right side. That's how real He is to me.

If you will believe God for it, He will reveal Himself to you just as surely and just as personally as He did to the prophets of old. Later John saw us reunited with Christ for eternity. Somehow, in that day, His presence will be so much more real.

The Crystal In John's Revelation

And before the throne there was a sea of glass like unto crystal ... .
                                                                         Revelation 4:6

Just as Ezekiel had seen us as crystal, John saw us as a *sea of glass* before the throne of God. The difference is that Ezekiel saw us as *terrible crystal.* He saw us shining forth from great darkness and triumphing in terrible times. John, on the other hand, sees us reflecting the glory of God's throne. Nothing reflects brilliant light more effectively than fine crystal.

The Living Stone and the Lively Stones In John's Revelation

And immediately I was in the spirit: and, behold, a throne was set in heaven, and one sat on the throne. And he that sat was to look upon like a jasper and a sardine stone: and there was a rainbow round about the throne, in sight like unto an emerald.   Revelation 4:2-3

Just as Ezekiel saw Christ as a stone and us as precious stones in His sight, John had the same revelation. Christ is precious; and, having partaken of His nature, we also become precious in the sight of God.

Another comparison worthy of mention is that of the eyes which both Ezekiel and John saw.

> *... and in the midst of the throne, and round about the throne, were four beasts FULL OF EYES before and behind.*   Revelation 4:6

> *And the four beasts had each of them six wings about him; and they were FULL OF EYES within ... .*   Revelation 4:8

> *As for their rings, they were so high that they were dreadful; and their rings were FULL OF EYES round about them four.*
> Ezekiel 1:18

Both the creatures and the beasts were FULL OF EYES. This must be significant. When we are taken by God into His realm, He gives us a special kind of sight. We no longer have just two eyes with limited vision. We have eyes *before and behind*. We have eyes *within*. We have eyes *round about* us. No enemy can creep up on us from the rear. God has given us special insight. We can see as He sees. We are *full of eyes*.

That doesn't mean I have to know and understand everything. Often I must walk by faith.

Once God gave me a vision of myself. I saw myself walking along on a paved road in the midst of some rolling hills, much like the foothills you see as you go past Calgary toward the Rockies. I was walking as fast as I once did as a young person. The way was not easy. It wound up and down the hills. When, I saw myself pause and look back, I heard the Lord say to me: "You will not always see the way before you, but you will always see it behind you." That knowledge has sustained me many times. I don't need to know exactly where I am going. When I walk with the Lord, step by step — by faith — I can always know that He has a purpose in mind. At some point, I will be able to look back and see it all clearly.

Sometimes I must walk by faith, but many times God wants to show me what lies ahead. He has given me eyes *before and behind*.

The Conclusion

I am grateful to God for the insight He has given me into the prophecies of Ezekiel and others. Ezekiel especially has been such a blessing to my own personal life and ministry. While visiting St. Paul's Cathedral in London, I was looking up into the dome and saw the painting of the four major prophets: Isaiah, Jeremiah, Ezekiel and Daniel. I looked at the artist's rendering of Ezekiel for a long time. Then I said, "Ezekiel, I just know you don't look like that." I feel like I know the man, and my concept of what he looks like is very different from that painting.

But, whatever he looks like, I thank God for a man who was willing to open himself to *visions of God* and to receive an *express* word from the Lord. One day I will personally thank him.

John's revelation has blessed me, as well, and I am grateful. The message of Revelation is a message to the Church.

> *He that hath an ear, let him hear what the Spirit saith unto the churches ... .*   Revelation 2:7, 11, 17, 29 and 3:13

These great prophetic books were considered mysteries by the church for many centuries. Today, because we are living in the last days, God is opening our understanding to these great truths. When John opened his heart to God, he heard God say to him, *"Come up hither, and I will shew thee things which must be hereafter"* (Revelation 4:1). Many generations have come and gone since these men of special insight passed away. Yet, somehow I hear the Spirit of God saying to us today: **Come up hither, and I will shew thee things which must be hereafter.** Amen!   ✳